THE ITALIANS IN AUSTR.

The Italians comprised the first truly la
arrived from Southern Europe after World War II. Today, people of Italian background in Australia number around one million. The Italians have made an enormous contribution to the development of Australian society through the twentieth century and to the present, and Gianfranco Cresciani – this country's foremost expert on Italian life in Australia – provides the definitive account. In this new edition Cresciani brings to life the important story of the Italo-Australian community into the twenty-first century.

Gianfranco Cresciani was born in Trieste, Italy and emigrated to Australia in 1962. He has researched the history of Italian migration to Australia since 1971, and is the author of many books on Italian culture including *Fascism, Anti-Fascism and Italians in Australia 1922–1945* and was the editor of *Australia, the Australians and the Italian Migration*. He is currently the general manager of infrastructure development within the Ministry for the Arts in New South Wales.

Migrants waiting to board ship in Naples, 1910.
(Italian Touring Club Archives)

THE ITALIANS IN AUSTRALIA

GIANFRANCO CRESCIANI

CAMBRIDGE
UNIVERSITY PRESS

For Jane, Emilio and Raffaella

"I believe in a multicultural society for Australia as unavoidable and desirable. It pains me to remember the chronic boredom of the predominantly Anglo-Saxon Australia of my youth. When I returned to live in the country after World War II, the presence of so-called ethnics is what made it bearable, and since then, their contributions have made life increasingly interesting."
(Patrick White to Geoffrey Blainey, letter, 1984, quoted in the *Sydney Morning Herald,* 8 November 2002)

"Australia is my home ... Italy my place of nostalgia".
(Franco Belgiorno-Nettis)

"To lose is part of our destiny. To lose your country is painful, but sometimes it can be normal, even healthy. All depends from the reasons which compelled you to leave, and the manner in which it was done, from your age or even from the season. The country in which you landed is not your Motherland, the country which you left ceases from being it, except in your memory. Your vision is disjointed between *us* and *them,* between *there* and *here*, between *once* and *now*. You have to wrestle with life before and life now: between discontinuity and nostalgia".
(Predrag Matvejević, author of *Mediterraneo*)

"Continuing a family tradition of migrations, I share without any effort the destiny of two or three different countries. I mistrust the cosy metaphors and when someone is telling me that man must have roots, my reply is that only trees must have roots. And anyhow, if one must deal with metaphors, why roots and not wings?"
(Juan Octavio Prenz, Argentinian writer of Istrian and Croatian background)

PUBLISHED BY THE PRESS SYNDICATE OF THE UNIVERSITY OF CAMBRIDGE
The Pitt Building, Trumpington Street, Cambridge, United Kingdom

CAMBRIDGE UNIVERSITY PRESS
The Edinburgh Building, Cambridge CB2 2RU, UK
40 West 20th Street, New York, NY 10011–4211, USA
477 Williamstown Road, Port Melbourne, VIC 3207, Australia
Ruiz de Alarcón 13, 28014 Madrid, Spain
Dock House, The Waterfront, Cape Town 8001, South Africa

http://www.cambridge.org

© Gianfranco Cresciani 2003

This book is copyright. Subject to statutory exception
and to the provisions of relevant collective licensing agreements,
no reproduction of any part may take place without
the written permission of Cambridge University Press.

First published 2003

Printed in Australia by Ligare Pty Ltd

Typeface Life Roman (*Adobe*) 10/16 pt.   *System* QuarkXPress® [PC]

A catalogue record for this book is available from the British Library

National Library of Australia Cataloguing in Publication data

Cresciani, Gianfranco, 1940– .
The Italians in Australia.
Rev. ed.
Bibliography.
Includes index.
ISBN 0 521 53778 9.
1. Italians – Australia – History. 2. Immigrants –
Australia. 3. Australia – Social life and customs.
I. Title.
994.00451

ISBN 0 521 53778 9 paperback

CONTENTS

Foreword	ix
Acknowledgements	xiii
1 A Country of Emigrants	1
2 Italians Discover Australia 1788–1900	26
3 The Italian Presence 1900–1940	51
4 Fascism and Anti-Fascism 1922–1940	73
5 Italians and Australians at War 1940–1947	97
6 Mass Migration 1945–1971	119
7 Full Circle	151
Select Bibliography	180
Index	184

FOREWORD

I first met Gianfranco Cresciani late in 1969. I was just back from a Cambridge PhD. My Harris Tweed sports coat and college tie demonstrated the fact. Although I was on the way to devoting my life to the understanding of modern Italy, the process was pretty incomplete. I had been raised in the deeply bourgeois North Shore of Sydney. Despite my pretensions to leftist politics, I accepted as natural that the local golf club to which I was joined at the age of 17 still banned Jews and Catholics from its membership lists. I had lived in Rome for a while in 1967–68 and knew some Italian academics. But Gianfranco Cresciani was my first real Italian friend and my first alerting to what would come to be called multicultural Australia.

Cresciani wrote an honours thesis and then a very distinguished MA under my supervision. The latter can be read in Italian or English version as the book *Fascism, Anti-fascism and Italians in Australia 1922–1945*. The MA would have been a PhD but for the predictably purblind regulations which then said that such a degree could only be done full-time. Cresciani, as a married and early mature-age student, worked for a living, and did his research 'part-time'. And so an MA it was.

I mention this matter not to claim any responsibility for the quality and extent of the research which Cresciani did. What was happening was one of those wonderful events for a youthful academic where I had happened on a 'student' whose destiny it was to teach me. And so, as our friendship continued and survived, I learned many things. I learned about Italy. I learned about the Italies. I learned about humankind. Cresciani was an immigrant from Trieste, that marvellously ambiguous city which stands at the junction of the Italian, German and Slav worlds, and not only them, since Cresciani's nickname while he was a *liceo* student was '*il turco*'—The Turk. One look at his photograph may tell you why. In Cresciani's very nature is embodied the impossibility of inscribing human beings into a single national or 'ethnic' category. The great Triestine novelist Italo Svevo remarked that 'it is the fate of humankind to live in mixed tenses', and this aphorism should be remembered whenever a Blainey, Howard or Hanson demands that we swear allegiance to 'one Australia'.

Despite his academic distinction Cresciani did not find a university job in 1970s Australia. Could the selection committees still have been composed of people with world views like those of my one-time North Shore golf club? Whatever the case, Cresciani worked for a while for the Italo-Australian construction company EPT, and then took office in the New South Wales bureaucracy where he has been a major figure in the building of cultural relations with Italy and with many other countries. All the time he went on being a historian (EPT's generosity to an employee who wished to involve himself in cultural pursuits still leaves me open-mouthed. If only mainstream Australian businesspersons could be persuaded that there is something beyond the bottom line apart from sporting endeavour).

Cresciani's pertinacity was extraordinary. I readily admit to loving the feel of archives, the dust under the fingernails, the sudden joy of a tiny detail on which my wordsmithery can start to work. But I usually have the pleasure of burying myself in the state archives in Rome, where there are catalogues and assistants and a little coffee shop just outside the fascist building which houses the *Archivio Centrale dello Stato*. In his determination to write the history of

Italians in Australia, Cresciani had to find the documents for himself. Since Australian historians and Australian archivists were themselves long dismally monolingual, they had done almost nothing to chart histories which were literally beyond their ken, or should I say beyond their kith and kin even in imagination. For years the 'Cresciani archive' would be the only serious place for anyone to research on Italo-Australia.

Cresciani also had to put up with simplicities in a literature which did expand under the impulse of the financial and status opportunities that arose with governmental multiculturalism. At least one Australian historian of Italians in this country seemed to think that their character was determined by something called the 'Italian Big Mamma'. Many 'community historians', lying for their old nation in a manner that was still less restrained than is true with many national historians, unreflectingly preached 'filio-pietism' and 'Whiggery'. Their versions of the history of Italo-Australia had it starting small but getting ever bigger. Their 'Pioneers' were unsullied Heroes (they were generally boys) who passed on a torch of national grandeur to a succession of Great or Important Men. One such chronicler even thought that Marco Polo might have a case to be hailed as the 'Father' of Italo-Australia on the somewhat specious grounds that he had gone to China to discover spaghetti and China was not so far away from Oz. He and his colleagues wrote the sort of history which might have satisfied a Giovanni Howard had he existed; in their view no black armbands need sully a green-white-and-red glory transported here to the Antipodes.

Cresciani had no time for such crudities, with their appalling insult to the precarious and changing character of the human condition. His work had begun with an exploration of fascism and anti-fascism on Australian soil. He therefore knew that migrants never compose innocently united, primordial and eternal 'communities'. He knew too that in a group of human beings, however constituted, power, in one form or another, will always be exercised. Just occasionally this power will be harnessed for the general good. Most often it will not. History itself is perennially a prey to the same dilemma. Should it accept its more obvious paymasters and fall to the task of propaganda, to the job of hedging around the fortress of the rich and rapacious with words? Or should it remained pledged to the cause of 'criticism, criticism, again criticism and criticism once more', as a major scholar who had seen meaning in 'Auschwitz' once urged? Cresciani, an anti-fascist historian to his bootstraps, has remained loyal to the second definition of our discipline. I share it with him and would like to think that it is what justifies the existence of historians in any society.

It is therefore an enormous pleasure and honour for me to welcome in this foreword the republication of Cresciani's history of *Italians in Australia*. When it first came out in 1985, it was a 'book of the film', Cresciani's ABC documentary, still far and away the best visual account of our migrant history. Now it has been amplified and reworked. Readers who cherish their commitment to liberty, equality and sorority will enjoy Cresciani's depiction of the travails and triumphs of people who migrated to Australia from both Italy and the Italies. Like us, these were people in transition, with identities which were both visceral and yet never wholly set. Like us, they did and did not possess free will. Like us, they were and were not Others. Their story teaches that national identity is always an oxymoron, one of those great oxymorons through which the human spirit in its glorious and loving ambiguity can survive even the troubles of the early twenty-first century. Through our knowledge of the patterns of such identity over time, we may yet be able to hymn our place as citizens of the world.

R. J. B. Bosworth
University of Western Australia

ACKNOWLEDGEMENTS

When I was invited by Cambridge University Press to work on a revised edition of *The Italians*, which I published in 1985 with ABC Enterprises, I wondered what would make the book more relevant, more topical to the contemporary reader. I reflected on the events of the last eighteen years that have given a different connotation to the history of Italy and of Italian emigration abroad. In doing so, I also recalled the people who had a lasting influence on my vision of the Italian migratory diaspora.

Two events in particular highlight the changed world and the new reality facing Italians who migrated many years ago across the oceans, to faraway countries, including Australia. One is the assent, given by the Commonwealth of Australia on 4 April 2002, that Australians of Italian background can regain their Italian nationality without losing the Australian one and thus maintain dual citizenship. This is an important acknowledgement of the contribution given by Italian migrants to their country of election, as well as recognition by Australian society of the importance of their cultural heritage—a novel, big step since 1985.

The second event is the widening, on 13 December 2002, of the European Union from fifteen to twenty-five member countries, thus creating a superpower of 455 million people. From this day, the Italian migrant overseas, thanks to his or her recently acquired dual citizenship, is also a member of the Union, a legal *cives orbis*, a citizen of the (European) world.

These legal and political milestones, as well as the profound social and economic changes in Italian and Australian society, have prompted me to largely rewrite the last two chapters of the book and to review, update and add new information to the others. To write about migration history means to span over the history of two countries, of many cultural *milieux*, of a plurality of micro histories hidden behind the events described by 'official' history, by macro history. It means, most of all, to speak out on facts and events conveniently forgotten or wilfully ignored by historians in the country of departure as well as the country of arrival.

Therefore, I am indebted, in the first place, to all Italian migrants who, during my thirty-two years of research in this area, have graciously agreed to be interviewed by me, to share with me their experiences, to entrust to me their memorabilia, photographs, records and documents, to make it possible for me to tell their tale, in my attempt to carve for them a rightful place in the historiography of Australia as well as of Italy.

In the second place, I owe a great debt of gratitude to three people who, over many decades, guided, helped and spurred me to go on writing on migration history. Richard J. Bosworth, unquestionably the most authoritative Australian scholar on contemporary Italy, from the beginning has been a valued friend, a trusted adviser, a helpful critic, an example to follow. The late Renzo De Felice, the Italian authority on Mussolini and Fascism, taught me that it was possible, indeed a duty, to historicise that *mondo dei vinti* (world of the vanquished), to salvage from neglect the history of those Italians outside Italy, to 'subvert' the comfortable interpretations of official historiography. The late Gianfausto Rosoli, the humble Scalabrinian priest who dedicated his life to unearth the history of Italians who migrated to other continents, taught me the unique historical value of each migrant experience, its centrality to the global economy of migration history.

Also, I wish to reiterate here my sincere appreciation for the assistance received from all staff of ABC Enterprises involved in 1985 with the first edition of *The Italians*, in particular to Glenn Hamilton for spurring me to write this book and to Helen Findlay and Nina Riemer for editing the text; to Leigh Nankervis for her professional graphic art work; to my research assistant, Belinda Mason, for her dedication in patiently and unrelentingly tracking down throughout Australia information and historical evidence which otherwise would not have been discovered; to Lloyd Capps, Christopher McCullough and Julie Cottrell-Dormer for affording me their invaluable collaboration. Sue Silversmith merited special mention for her efficiency in getting the then almost illegible manuscript into a presentable state for the publishers.

To the staff of Cambridge University Press, in particular to Amanda Pinches, Peter Debus, Paul Watt, Karen Hildebrandt and Kim Armitage, I extend my special thanks for their support, editorial assistance and invaluable suggestions to bring to the press in 2003 this revised edition of the book. I am also greatly indebted to Venetia Somerset, who has painstakingly edited the revised text and offered valued advice to enrich it. However, the merit of thinking of a new edition, and the drive to make it possible goes exclusively to Angelo Loukakis, publishing Consultant of Cambridge University Press Australia. To my dear friend Angelo go my heartfelt thanks.

Sincere thanks are also due to Professor Richard Bosworth of the University of Western Australia, who gracefully consented to write the Foreword to this volume.

ACKNOWLEDGEMENTS

The publishers and I would like to thank the following individuals and organisations for their permission to reproduce material which appears in the book. Every reasonable effort has been made to trace the copyright-holders. Where this has not been possible we apologise to those concerned: Archivi Alinari, Florence; Archivio Fotografico Comunale, Rome; Mario Nunes Vais Collection; Istituto Centrale per il Catalogo e la Documentazione, Rome; P. Becchetti; Museo Civico Castello Sforzesco, Milan, Collezione Bertarelli; Museo Centrale del Risorgimento, Rome; Italian Touring Club; Centro Studi Emigrazione, Rome; Congregazione della Propaganda Fide, Rome; New Norcia Museum, Western Australia; Diocesan Archives, Armidale; Mitchell Library, Sydney; Richmond River Historical Society; Biblioteca Feltrinelli, Milan; National Library of Australia, Canberra; John Oxley Library of Queensland; *Western Mail*; *Bollettino dell'Emigrazione*; Italian Historical Society, Melbourne; Water Resources Commission, Sydney; *West Australian*; *Italo-Australian*; Istituto Luce, Rome; Archivio Centrale dello Stato, Rome; *Italian Bulletin of Australia*; New York Public Library; Australian War Memorial, Canberra; *Sydney Morning Herald*; *Oggi*; *L'Espresso*; *The Economist*; Agenzia ANSA, Italy; Ted Bader; Alfredo Garipoli; Camillo Di Rocco; Giovanna Borgese; Transfield Group of Industries.

Finally, to my wife Jane, son Emilio and daughter Raffaella, I want to express my heartfelt gratitude for their constant support and patience in giving me time to rewrite this book and somehow relive the Italian migrant experience.

1
A COUNTRY OF EMIGRANTS

From time immemorial, Italy, La Bella Italia, has attracted and mesmerised the foreigners lured to her shores for different and often contrasting reasons. Invaders and conquerors, from Hannibal to Hitler, descended on the peninsula by crossing the Alps, or raided her long and undefended coastline, dazzled by the fertility of the land, the beauty of the climate, the riches which could be plundered from her population.

For 2000 years pilgrims and religious reformers, from Luther to Lefebvre, have flocked to Rome and to other places of devotion to question or strengthen their faith, to scourge the Church or to pay homage to the cradle of Christianity. Artists and writers from many countries carried out their intellectual pilgrimage to this land, to draw on her vibrant heritage for their inspiration: Joyce, Ruskin, Goethe, Stendhal, Thomas Mann, Byron, Shelley, Keats and Maxim Gorky were among the many literati who lived in Italy and were influenced markedly in their work by the experience. Revolutionaries like Lenin, anarchists like Bakunin, poets like Ezra Pound—all visited and felt attracted by this ancient, complex and in many ways, unfathomable country, by its people, its culture, its politics.

CROWN LANDS AND EMIGRATION.

AUSTRALIA.

"WHY DOST THOU WRONG HER, THAT DID NE'ER WRONG THEE?"

WHEN Great Britain founded the Colony of New South Wales, it was with no financial objects; she sought in doing so to relieve herself, not of the *expense*, but of the *presence* of her convicts.

Had these criminals been retained at home, Great Britain must have increased, at an enormous outlay, the number of her prisons and houses of correction; and the expense besides of maintaining the prisoners within them would have been greater than has been created by every branch of service in the Australian Colonies*.

The former course would have been not merely barren and unproductive in its results, but would have been attended with the serious evil of a constant return of criminals to the bosom of society, whence they have been expelled: the latter mode has given birth and permanent establishment to no less than two valuable Colonies, with all the commercial advantages which flow from their connexion with the parent state†.

The first settlers in those Colonies were the families of the naval, military, and civil officers, by whom the social institutions of a civilized community were there maintained.

The Government of Great Britain gave to them grants of land, with convict servants to assist in its cultivation, or to occupy with flocks and herds the native pastures which it affords.

Without such aid, the land would not have been worth acceptance. The labour, however, so afforded, was not altogether gratuitous; in return for it, Great Britain was relieved of a heavy expense in feeding and clothing the convicts, whose services she had assigned to private persons.

Between the Colonists and the Mother Country there may be said then to have been a balance of advantage, equally beneficial to the one party and the other.

If Great Britain furnished such labour as could be derived from her convicts, let it be remembered, on the other hand, that it was by means of the sagacity, the enterprise, and perseverance of the Colonists, giving to that labour its true direction, that it was turned to good account; it was by their means, principally, that the Colony was raised from the depth of moral debasement into which it would have sunk; and instead of the mere penitentiary which, but for them, it must have become, these Colonists gave to it almost whatever is good of the character, and much of the value which it now possesses.

The system of free grants of land, with assignment of convicts as servants, continued in force until about the year 1830, by which time many of the subjects of Great Britain had emigrated to the Australian Colonies, and there embarked their fortunes under direct encouragement of Government, and allured by the advantages which this its line of policy afforded.

---

* The nett expense of five several mode of confinement or treatment of criminals in England is as follows:—

	£. s. d.
In the Hulks	7 14 2
Boys in the Euryalus Hulk	13 5 6¼
Cold Bath Fields House of Correction	13 15 2
Wakefield ditto	14 0 3¼
Milbank Penitentiary	24 6 6
	5)73 1 7¾

Giving a mean expenditure per ann. of £14 12 3⅜

In England and Wales in 1837 there were sentenced to death 438, executed 8, remaining 430
Transported for life 636
   ,,   15 years 66
   ,,   14 do. 479
   ,,   10 do. 179
   ,,   7 do. 2413
                                                        4203

It may be fairly assumed that the entire number would have remained a charge to the State during seven years, constituting an expense of more than 100*l.* each. Since the establishment of the Australian Colonies about 111,000 persons have been transported to them.

Had these criminals been retained in England, the charge for their maintenance alone could not have been less than 11,100,000*l.*

Seven years are assumed as the mean term of imprisonment, under a belief, that if the public welfare, blended with mercy, is to be the rule, and not convenience or a temporary expediency, a less term cannot be adopted.

† The proportionate value of this connexion is estimated to be in the ratio of five to one beyond that of the commerce of Great Britain with any foreign people; so that the advantage she derives from 100,000 people in Australia is equal to that of 500,000 on the Continent of Europe.

Surely such an harvest would amply repay the labour and cost of sowing. It is not to the vain endeavour to regain old markets, but to create new, by means of the energies of her own subjects, that Great Britain should now apply herself.

A pamphlet promoting emigration from the British Isles to Australia, 1840. The document claims that 'no one who is able and willing to labour need want the necessities or convenience of life; the poor are conveyed thither in safety, comfort, and precision, and what to them is of vast moment, without expense. The promotion of emigration, therefore, to this quarter, it will be seen, is a work of the most enlightened charity'. (Cresciani Collection)

Today, according to data collected in 1997 by the Italian Institute of Statistics (ISTAT), over 56 million tourists (207 000 of whom are Australian) go to Italy annually in a peaceful invasion, to enjoy her cultural life, her cuisine and folklore, her beautiful holiday resorts, the incomparable landscape, the extrovert and uninhibited way of life of her inhabitants. Some still see today's Italy as the land of classicism, of Rome and her empire, as the centre of that great tradition which, together with Greece, moulded what we today call Western Civilisation. To many, Italy means the Roman Catholic Church, faith, the spiritual inspiration experienced by being in Rome, by seeing the Pope, by visiting the Vatican or the Catacombs, by having, even for a few days, an unforgettable religious experience. Other people are attracted rather by the great secular tradition, by the cultural achievements of Italy, by the Renaissance, by the

Giuseppe Garibaldi, soon after being wounded at Aspromonte, with his wife, Francesca Armosino, and a daughter. (Archivio Fotografico Comunale, Rome)

splendour of imperial Venice, by the glittering cultural life of fifteenth- and sixteenth-century Florence, Mantua, Pisa, Ferrara, Urbino, by the entrepreneurial acumen of Grand Ducal Milan, whose bankers at that time controlled European finance.

To modern tourists and to foreigners in general, Italy's best image is her past. The present, as far as they are concerned, does not even exist. Or, if scant notice is being taken of Italy's contemporary life, the stereotypes about her present are rather less noble and dignified. For instance, contemporary Italy is perceived as a country ruled by the Mafia, beset by governmental instability, haunted by political terrorism, plagued by the problem of a poverty-stricken South, as a land inhabited by an unruly, arrogant, boisterous, garlic-smelling, melodic 'race' of people, who, given the chance, are eager to emigrate to countries enjoying a superior, more orderly and sedate standard of living. Thus the dominant value-judgement of Italy expressed by many people is conditioned by the seemingly inexplicable and puzzling dichotomy between Italy's undeniably glorious past and her allegedly confused and turbulent present.

The reality is much more complex than the prevailing clichés and cannot be understood by looking into just one of the many facets of the prism. Italy is like a stage where, if one only looks at the performance taking place in the foreground, one can easily miss the importance of what happens backstage. Commonly held beliefs, for instance that Italy is a very old country and that the 'Italians' from long past are a homogeneous people, under closer scrutiny manifest their precariousness unless they are related to the general trend of Italian history.

Instead, Italy, like Australia, notwithstanding the many layers of civilisations—Sannite, Etruscan, Greco-Roman, Byzantine, Renaissance, Baroque, Neoclassical—is a relatively young nation having achieved independence and Unification by 17 March 1861.

The breach of Porta Pia seen from Villa Patrizi. In September 1870 Italian troops entered Rome through the breach of Porta Pia, effectively ending the Pope's temporal power. In July 1871 the Eternal City was declared capital of the Kingdom of Italy. (Istituto Centrale per il Catalogo e la Documentazione, Rome)

Since the Middle Ages, the history of Italy had been one of divisions, of struggles between local factions which often sought aid from 'foreigners' in order to overcome and dominate their neighbours. It was a history of conflicts between Guelphs and Ghibellines, of city-state against city-state, of principate against principate, of Florence against Pisa, of Venice against Genoa, of 'Italians' against 'Italians'. For centuries this divisiveness, which some social scientists have described as a characteristic of the Italian people, was exploited by other nations and Italy became the battleground for their ambitions, a pawn in the game of power-politics for European supremacy played by the Great Powers.

Indeed, Italy was expendable, and the cluster of small states which characterised the political geography of the peninsula at the beginning of the nineteenth century was the outcome of that Yalta-style settlement which had been agreed upon at the Congress of Vienna in 1815, where the Austrian Prince Metternich contemptuously declared that Italy was a mere geographic expression. Before 1861, Italy was indeed a 'geographic expression', a conglomerate of vassal states, subservient to the superpowers of Europe.

To the north-west the Kingdom of Sardinia, under the Savoy dynasty, was an uneasy buffer state between France and the north-eastern provinces of Lombardy and Veneto, since 1815 under

Group of southern brigands captured near Salerno by the Italian Army in July 1865. (P. Becchetti, Fotografi e Fotografia in Italia. 1839–1880, Rome 1978)

Austrian occupation. The Duchies of Parma and Modena were simply sinecures for members of the Austrian imperial family, and hosted Austrian garrisons. The Grand Duchy of Tuscany, ruled by offspring of the House of Lorraine, was also under the political influence of Austria, and the same can be said, to a large extent, for the Papal States which occupied today's regions of Marche, Lazio, Umbria, Abruzzi and part of the Emilia. To the south, the Kingdom of the Two Sicilies was ruled by the Bourbons, who had the unenviable fame of being the least enlightened and intelligent monarchs on the market.

Unquestionably, before Unification, political power in these small states lay in the hands of their reactionary rulers, who tried to turn back the clock of history and restore in the peninsula regimes, ideas and policies which the French Revolution had effectively destroyed. Considering the political fragmentation and the disruptive influence exercised by the Great European powers, at that time no fair-minded European ever seriously thought that Italy would achieve unification. It was common belief that Italians did not seek unification, indeed, that there were no Italians as such, but a conglomeration of Piedmontese, Genoese, Romans, Venetians, who all spoke their own dialect, had their own distinctive culture, looked after their sectarian interests and were quite busy seeing that their rivals across the border would not outmatch them in economic, military and political influence.

Italian, as a language, was a minority language (as indeed it is even today, most Italians preferring to speak their own dialect). British historian Denis Mack Smith claims that in 1860 only 4 per cent of people spoke Italian, whereas Latin was still a language frequently used by the intellectual elite. Absent from the peninsula's historical experience were the profound cultural, social, economic and political upheavals of the Reformation, with its revolutionary

Multiculturalism ante litteram. *Private Iacob Hrešcăk, of Trieste, Slovene, profession carter, at the outbreak of World War I, in August 1914, is drafted in the 97th Infantry Regiment Freiherr von Waldstatten of the Austro-Hungarian Army. The photo was taken by an Italian photographer. Hrešcăk was killed in 1917 on the Italian front by an Italian explosive device. Iacob's son, Ivan, served in the early 1920s in the* Bersaglieri *corps of the Italian Army, and his grandson emigrated to Australia in 1962.*
(Cresciani Collection)

impact as far as trade, business, individual interaction and ethics were concerned. Instead, the stifling cloak of the Counter Reformation characterised the intellectual and political life of the country. Italy was (and still is) a nation which had not experienced the disruption of a revolution, but was (and still is) the country of compromise, of doubtful alliances, of *compromessi storici*—historical compromises—where *bisogna tirare avanti*—life must go on irrespectively—because *le cose si fanno da sè*—things adjust themselves.

To this dismal picture of political reality we must add another, no less disheartening picture of the social and economic conditions of the country. With the exception of a few industrial complexes in the north, namely the textile industry and wool industry at Biella and Schio, there was no viable industrial structure in the country. The Industrial Revolution came to most of Italy as late as the beginning of the twentieth century, long after Great Britain, France, Germany and Belgium had achieved their revolutions. Communications were extremely poor, given the geography of the country, its political divisions and the countless tariff barriers, and trade was still in its infancy. By 1848 Italy had only 265 kilometres of railway lines, and only in 1840 was the first Italian shipping line, the Raffaele Rubattino, founded in Genoa. Illiteracy was extremely high. In 1861, 90 per cent of the inhabitants of the peninsula could not read or write. Agriculture in many regions was still in an undeveloped, subsistence state, barely satisfying the needs of the inhabitants.

There was no militant workers' movement which could be even remotely compared to the Chartists in England. There was no sizable middle class to cushion the inaction of a reactionary ruling class and to express in a forceful and effective way the political needs of large sections of the population. There were indeed two societies, vastly different, two countries: the *paese legale* represented by the ruling class and its supporters, and the *paese reale* comprising the larger part of Italian society. There were rulers and ruled, exploiters and exploited (then as today), with the difference that then there were no channels through which the demands and the aspirations of most of the population could be legally transmitted to the rulers. How, then, given this depressing situation, was Unification achieved, and what were the forces striving for it? Why and how did they succeed? Or did they succeed at all?

In effect the Unification of Italy was the end result of many components: the visionary idealism of a small band of intellectuals and revolutionaries; the determination of one state, the Piedmontese Kingdom of Sardinia, to achieve a centuries-old Machiavellian dream of a prince imposing his military and political hegemony over

Women carrying stones, c. 1900. Conditions of employment in preindustrial nineteenth-century Italy were harsh and often dehumanising. The peasantry, which represented the bulk of the labour force, had to endure long working hours and physically debilitating tasks. (Istituto Centrale per il Catalogo e la Documentazione, Rome)

the rest of the country; the complex struggle for supremacy of the European Great Powers, which the Italians partly exploited to their advantage, and of which they were the lucky beneficiaries.

To a large extent, the political fate of Italy was inexorably linked to the whims and turns of European Great Power politics, irrespective of the wishes of her rulers and inhabitants. It is indeed ironic, but by no means historically irrelevant, that Piedmont increased its territorial control over most of the peninsula in spite of repeated and crushing military defeats at the hands of the Austrian Army and Navy, as at Novara in 1849 and at Custoza and Lissa in 1866. Thus Unification was the successful product of diplomatic manoeuvring and military interplay orchestrated by Vienna, Paris and London and by a small band of 'Italians', while the vast majority of the peasantry stood by watching impassively, apathetically or even antagonistically, at this alleged political awakening, at this Risorgimento of Italy.

Italian political hagiography claims four people as the main architects of the Risorgimento: the Piedmontese King Victor Emmanuel II; his Premier Camillo Benso, Count Cavour; flamboyant adventurer, sailor and soldier Giuseppe Garibaldi; and the standard-bearer of messianic, revolutionary republicanism, Giuseppe Mazzini.

King Victor Emmanuel II, canonised by Italian nationalist historiography as the *re galantuomo*, the 'gentleman king', but better known as the *re galante*, the 'randy king', given his sexual safaris among the peasant womenfolk of Piedmont, was only interested in playing the old game of exploiting the conflicting interests of France and Austria to his own advantage. He saw Unification as a process whereby Piedmont would extend its control over as much as possible of the rest of Italy, and an indication of his attitude is given by

King Victor Emmanuel II with his wife, 'La bella Rosina' (Foto Alinari)

The Bersaglieri fire on the demonstrators. Social and political unrest, caused by the worsening economic conditions, was endemic at the end of the nineteenth century. During the bread riots which took place in Milan between 6 and 9 May 1898, the troops of General Fiorenzo Bava-Beccaris shot and killed 200 people. (Museo Civico Castello Forzesco, Milan. Collezione Bertarelli)

the fact that after Unification he did not even bother to change his dynastic name of Victor Emmanuel II, King of Sardinia, to the more fitting one of King Victor Emmanuel I of Italy. Also, he moved the capital, very reluctantly, from Turin to the unhealthy climate of Rome where in 1878 he died from malaria or perhaps, as the gossipers of the royal court insinuated, from sheer exhaustion after his marriage with 'La bella Rosina', allegedly a well-known practitioner of the oldest profession in the world. It is also indicative that both Victor Emmanuel and his Prime Minister, Camillo Benso, were French-educated and could speak only very basic Italian.

Camillo Benso was another kind of man. Well educated, a skilful politician, open to demands for reform, he was the main architect of Piedmont's foreign policy, a policy which paid Piedmont handsomely. It was Count Cavour who put the 'Italian question' to the fore of the European Chancelleries, who sent Italian troops to the Crimean War in 1854 in order to have Piedmont sitting at the peace conference, on a par with France, Great Britain and Austria. His scheming brought about the Unification of Italy, although Cavour never thought of an Italy united from the Alps to Sicily, but only a kingdom of northern-central Italy. Indeed, later on, he considered the acquisition of southern Italy as a mistake, given the underdeveloped conditions of those regions, thus beginning that animosity of Northerners towards Southerners that is crystallised in the hostile dictum that Africa begins south of Rome.

Instead, the southern regions of Italy were annexed to the Kingdom of Italy in 1860 when they were conquered by 1000 redshirted irregular troops led by that nineteenth-century Che Guevara, Giuseppe Garibaldi. Garibaldi, an ardent idealist of republican sympathies and a freemason, later in his life espoused the monarchist cause, albeit reluctantly. A romantic nationalist and brilliant guerrilla fighter, his charismatic figure was the only one, among the leaders of the Risorgimento, which succeeded appreciably in rousing the enthusiasm of some sections of the Italian peasantry to the point that the indictment *ha parlato male di Garibaldi*—he has slandered Garibaldi—became an accusation equivalent to carrying out antinational activities. For many years, in the miserable huts and homes of the South, the portrait of Garibaldi figured prominently, side by side with those of the King and the Virgin Mary, only to be substituted in less happy times by that of another *condottiere*, Benito Mussolini.

A sailor by profession and a rebel by nature, 'intolerant of a sedentary existence', as he confessed in his memoirs, Garibaldi joined in 1833 the Giovine Italia (Young Italy), an underground revolutionary movement led by Giuseppe Mazzini, the ideologue of the Unification of Italy, and took part in the failed Mazzinian conspiracy in Genoa in 1834. He fled to South America, where from 1835 to 1848 he fought for the independence of Uruguay, Brazil and Argentina. For his guerrilla exploits in South America, as well as later on in Italy and France, he was dubbed by nationalist hagiographers the Hero of the Two Worlds. Garibaldi was the charismatic Italian representative of that band of romantic patriots, such as the Polish poet Adam Mitzkievich and the Hungarian Petöfi, who fought against reactionary European governments and for the independence of their and other countries.

The daring action, the unexpected raid, the partisan tactics were more his style than the conventional methods of warfare, and that was the reason Garibaldi was so successful militarily, even when the Piedmontese regular army was soundly defeated. For instance, in 1860 he landed at Marsala, in Sicily, and thrust himself and his 1000 red-shirted Garibaldini into an impulsive, irresponsible and incredibly successful adventure, without prior knowledge or intelligence information on the military, political and economic situation awaiting him. At times, reality was in conflict with his wishes. For example, some of the peasants who were supposedly anxiously awaiting the arrival of the Garibaldini in order to be liberated from tyranny and oppression sided with the reactionary Bourbons, fought against Garibaldi's men and were captured and executed by them.

Another agent of Italian nationalism was undoubtedly Giuseppe Mazzini who, with his republicanism and his revolutionary preaching, did much to galvanise young Italian intellectuals and idealists into action. The countless episodes of attempted uprisings against the established rulers, such as those of the Bandiera brothers and of Carlo Pisacane, are outstanding examples of his influence among thinking and educated Italians. It must be pointed out nevertheless

Ethnic Italians from Trieste drafted in the medical corps of the Austro-Hungarian Army, August 1914. (Cresciani Collection)

Italian troops cross the Austrian border. Italy declared war against the Central Powers on 24 May 1915. World War I would end with the annexation of Trento and Trieste and with massive social dislocation and widespread political unrest. (Museo Centrale del Risorgimento, Rome)

that these attempts were doomed to failure since there was, to use the Maoist phraseology, no sea in which the revolutionary fish could swim. In fact Pisacane and his followers were butchered by the very people they wanted to liberate, the peasants. Change and authority were two concepts repugnant to the mentality of the Italian masses, deeply suspicious of the educated and of people in power who, for centuries, had exploited them mercilessly.

The majority of the population remained cut off from the nationalist fervour expressed by the Piedmontese ruling elite and by the emerging bourgeoisie. Instead, the 'common people' were concerned mainly with their centuries-old problems of subsistence, of struggle against the unyielding land, the diseases and the natural elements, and of avoiding the authorities because they meant only taxes, vexations and discriminations. The only avenues open to them to escape this desperate situation were open rebellion or running away. In effect, brigandage and emigration became, after Unification, two social phenomena that left a deep mark on contemporary southern history and popular culture. The many peasant revolts that broke out in the south were a recurrent symptom of desperation, of peasant *Jacquerie*, not of nationalism. The degree of discontent and alienation among the southern peasants is indicated by the fact that after Unification, half of the Italian Army spent more than five years quelling peasant uprisings in the south, and the number of dead in those peasant wars exceeded that of the fallen during the wars of the Risorgimento.

Thus the Unification of Italy was an event thrust upon most Italians despite their wishes. It was a 'revolution from above', or, better still, to use the dictum coined by Communist leader and historian Antonio Gramsci, it was a *rivoluzione mancata*, a revolution which never took place. Everything changed to stay just the same as it had been before. Italy remained the land of the parochial, of the *faide di comune*, local feuds, where local interests played a much greater part than national interests and where a *galantuomo*, a *signore*, had more in common with his peers 1000 kilometres away than with the *contadini*, the peasants among whom he lived. The disparity between regions, between social classes, between different models of development in the country, the differences of language, customs, moral outlook, expectations, the heritage of centuries-old rivalries, hatreds, conflicting economic interests,

Emigrants entering a migrant's hostel in Milan before their departure for a new life. The hostel was managed by the Società Umanitaria, a Socialist organisation which, together with the Catholic Opera Bonomelli, was assisting people before embarkation. Omero Schiassi, the most prominent Italian anti-Fascist émigré in Australia, worked for the Umanitaria in 1902–3. (Italian Touring Club Archives)

would not be overcome by the forced extension of Piedmontese 'law and order' over the rest of the peninsula, and contributed significantly to alienating large sections of the population from their own country.

It is within this political, social and economic context that the tragic phenomenon of Italian mass migration took place whereby, between 1876 and 1976, more than 26 million Italians left their country in search of fortune elsewhere, an exodus which already in 1906 the Minister for Foreign Affairs, Tommaso Tittoni, admitted was a 'phenomenon abnormal in character and proportions'. Emigration was triggered by international as well as national causes.

Italian emigrants in Genoa board a ship bound for the Americas (c. 1890) (Mario Nunes Vais Collection)

During the second half of the nineteenth century new, developing countries like Argentina, Brazil and the United States began attracting large masses of foreign labour to assist in the colonisation and exploitation of their virgin lands and in the manning of their new and rapidly flourishing industrial and mining complexes. During 1883 alone, 800 000 Europeans emigrated to the Americas. Likewise, Italian manpower was attracted to France, Germany, Belgium and other European countries, to sustain these countries in the take-off stage of their Industrial Revolution.

Italians were also spurred to emigrate by reasons inherently local, seasonal or national in character. Unification had meant to most an increase in taxes, levied in order to pay for the Risorgimento wars. In particular, the infamous *tassa sul macinato*, the tax on the milling of wheat, imposed in 1868, had a devastating effect on the poorest classes in society. Furthermore, misleading propaganda by agents of the shipping companies and of foreign governments that, abroad, work was readily available and well remunerated, that a fortune could be made quickly in the American Eldorado, convinced countless northern and southern Italian peasants to sell their meagre belongings and to leave their country.

Besides, the sight of the dollars and the pesos sent by the migrants to their families still living in their impoverished villages had a spurring effect on the peasants who were still hesitant in taking the road to faraway countries. By the end of the nineteenth century, remittances from emigrants increased sharply, and were injecting into the Italian economy money badly needed to maintain that economic and social equilibrium which, if broken, would have unquestionably led to more peasant uprisings and to revolutionary attempts. While in 1900 remittances amounted to 246 million lire, by 1906 they had already risen to 880 million lire. Also, the economic depressions that hit Europe in 1882–85 and 1890–95 and the

A poster of the 12 567 tonne liner Kaiser Franz Joseph I, *launched at the Monfalcone shipyard in 1911. It was owned by the Cosulich family, trading under the name Austro-Americana Line. It started regular passenger and freight services from Trieste to South and North America and embarked emigrants in Trieste, Naples and Palermo. After the First World War, the Cosulich family restarted shipping activities with the trade name of Cosulich Line. The* Kaiser Franz Joseph I, *a name by then quite inappropriate, was renamed* President Wilson. (Cresciani Collection)

ensuing collapse of the international market price of agricultural products (one of the main items of export in the Italian balance of trade), accelerated the economic crisis in the Italian countryside. This crisis reached dramatic proportions in the south where badly needed reforms were not introduced, thus increasing the gap between its inefficient agricultural infrastructure and a north undergoing a rapid process of industrialisation and economic rationalisation. Investment in the south was also inadequate. In 1887 deposits in southern banks amounted to 272 million lire, while northern banks held more than 2135 million lire.

In addition, emigration was encouraged by the authorities because it constituted a safety valve against the rising tide of political unrest centred on the Socialist movement and the trade unions. It was

Migrants crammed on the deck of a ship crossing the Atlantic Ocean, 1898. (Centro Studi Emigrazione Archives, Rome)

earnestly hoped that the most disaffected people would prefer to take the road to emigration rather than that leading to social revolution. Already by 1876, the first year when statistical data were officially recorded, emigration had reached epidemic proportions. One of the more popular songs of the time was 'Dear Mother, give me a hundred lire, I want to go to America'. Year after year, hundreds of thousands of people began leaving Italy, forced by their desperate conditions or encouraged by news received from friends already emigrated. This exodus reached its peak in 1913 when 813 000 people, one in forty Italians, left the country.

Emigration became also a highly profitable business. Unscrupulous agents, shipping officers and petty bureaucrats soon found out that there was a lot of money to be made by exploiting the misery of the migrant. Migrants were often compelled to travel overseas under appalling conditions. Edoardo Pantano, an Italian Member of Parliament, reported in 1899 that Italian ship owners were making a handsome profit

> out of the loads of human flesh which they cram, crush, starve or mistreat on their old, rotting boats, with less consideration than if they were animals. The memory is still fresh and one does not know whether it is more shameful than pitiful, of some steamers, laden with human flesh, the route of which across the ocean was marked by a long trail of corpses of the weakest and sickest migrants, of women, of children, debilitated, destroyed by contaminated or insufficient food, by lack of medical care and, sad to say, by lack of fresh air.

Mercilessly swindled by shipping agents and on the way to being brutally exploited by greedy employers, migrants were driven like sheep across the ocean in ships which until a few years previously had been used for the black slave trade between Africa and the Americas. Boatloads were leaving from Genoa and Naples bound for Brazil, Argentina and the United States, with their miserable cargo travelling without any certainty of arriving at their destination. In 1884 the vessel *Matteo Bruzzo* left for Montevideo with 1333 passengers, but after three months on the seas and after having been chased out of Montevideo by gunfire, only a few survived, the rest being killed by cholera. In 1888 the *Cachar* reported thirty-seven victims from hunger and asphyxia and in 1894 the vessel *Carlo Raggio* had 206 dead from cholera and measles. Also in 1894, the *Andrea Doria* recorded 159 dead out of 1317 passengers.

Yet despite untold suffering, Italians continued to emigrate. Soon New York would become by far the largest Italian city, and Ellis Island, the gateway for Italians entering the United States, would witness a seemingly unending stream of people anxiously awaiting customs clearance to be allowed to enter the long dreamt-of Eldorado. Living in a foreign land, among foreign people, and having to cope with unfamiliar customs and languages, was often difficult. At times the Italian migrant was treated with hostility, discrimination and hatred and was even the target of violence. In 1891, at New Orleans in the United States, eleven Italians were lynched by a frenzied mob. In 1893 at Aigues Mortes, in France, French miners savagely attacked their Italian workmates, killing fifty and wounding 150. Soon, in almost every place where there was a sizable Italian migrant community, there sprang up little Italies and Italian clubs and associations aiming at sheltering Italians, at protecting them from the culture shock of living in an alien and hostile environment. The proliferation of these ethnic ghettoes exacerbated significantly the bad relations between migrants and their host society.

This situation of strident social conflict was most pronounced during periods of economic depression. After the First World War, which put an abrupt end to Italian emigration, the long period of economic crisis that hit most industrialised nations saw a decrease in the inflow of competitive migrant labour. In 1921 the United States imposed a quota system. Unable to continue to emigrate to that country, Italians began looking for other countries where they could go and work. Australia was one. Between 1922 and 1927 the number of Italian settlers in this country grew from 8500 to 33 000.

The advent of Fascism in Italy also contributed to restricting Italian emigration to other countries. Mussolini believed that it was humiliating and demeaning for Italians to go and work to the advantage of foreign countries, contributing to their wealth, growth and economic power. Instead he felt that Italians ought to go and develop the Italian colonies of Libya, Eritrea and Somalia, thus building the foundations of an Italian colonial empire. Il Duce's dream of a Second Roman Empire built on the back of the proletarian peasantry was shattered by the second world conflict. Ironically, the Italian conscript, who had traditionally gone to the United States, Canada, South Africa or Australia as a migrant, was transported to these countries as a prisoner of war. For instance over 18 000 Italian prisoners of war were held in Australian detention camps. After 1945, many would return as migrants to the countries which had hosted them behind barbed wire.

The reconstruction of Europe after the ravages of the war and the ensuing European economic recovery created the framework for a renewal of Italian migration abroad, as well as for massive internal migration within Italy. Italian peasants from the south not only went again to work in the Belgian coal mines, on the farms in France, in the German factories, or overseas, but 5 million of them migrated to northern Italy, to work in the Fiat car works at Turin, in the foundries of Reggio Emilia, in the petrochemical complexes of Milan and Porto Marghera, Venice.

The amazing economic recovery of Italy during the 1950s and 1960s, the 'Italian economic miracle', rapidly narrowed the economic gap with other countries. Thus, with the improvement in economic conditions, Italians felt less motivated to emigrate, to look for employment and fortune in foreign lands. Since the 1970s, social and material conditions as well as work opportunities became more or less similar throughout the European Economic Community. Italian industry and the Italian economy itself began importing foreign manpower, and today Italy hosts 2 300 000 legal immigrants, in addition to hundreds of thousands of illegal immigrants, who are employed mainly in agriculture and in the tertiary sector.

Today, Italians migrate no more. They have found their lucky country at home. Life, even in Italy, as former Australian Prime Minister Malcolm Fraser was fond of reminding us, is not meant to be easy, but to Italians it is a great deal easier in Italy than in a foreign land where discrimination, cultural alienation, social isolation and homesickness are usually the heavy price that a migrant has to pay in exchange for economic security. It is indeed a lot easier at home, among one's family, friends and foes, than in a faraway land, even when this land is called Australia.

2
ITALIANS DISCOVER AUSTRALIA 1788–1900

As well as the Age of Enlightenment, of Liberalism and of the Industrial Revolution, the late eighteenth century and the nineteenth century were the centuries in which Europe launched herself into the fascinating and challenging race of the last great world explorations. Improved technology in shipbuilding, transport and communications made possible the discovery of the yet unknown corners of the earth. This period also marked for the European Powers the last stage of imperial and colonial expansion. The struggle for supremacy shifted from the European theatre to Asia, Africa and Oceania, where the Great Powers competed with each other in their land-grabbing efforts by using different yet interrelated means: geographic expeditions, missionary presence, colonial settlements, economic exploitation, gunboat diplomacy and, ultimately, war.

The motivation for the philosophy that it was the white man's burden to bring his civilisation, culture and religion to the rest of the world lay in the principles of the Enlightenment, in the idea of progress. In reality, this lofty civilising mission, this urge to know, to possess and to change the world masked the more base and vulgar struggle for colonial expansion and imperial supremacy then being waged by the Great European Powers among themselves.

Italy, the least of the Great Powers, was slow to enter this exclusive contest for the world's last available real estate, because of the lateness of her Unification. The new Italian state, left with the crumbs of possible colonial acquisitions, was nevertheless able to establish at the end of the nineteenth century a colonial foothold in Eritrea and Somalia, stake its claim on Ethiopia and, later on, occupy Libya and the Dodecanese Islands and send a military garrison to Tientsin, China. Like other Great Powers, Italy also used the same excuses to justify her expansionism. Geographic explorations were promoted in the name of progress, to be followed by the establishment of missionary outposts in order to bring Christian civilisation to the heathen. The ensuing arrival of colonists, or migrants, was justified by the economic necessity to develop these lands, and the setting up of military garrisons could be explained by the need to protect the European settlements from the predictable hostility of the natives. Once this chain of events was set in motion, the colonial power believed she had valid reasons to serve the other European powers notice of her 'interests' in the area.

In the pursuit of such policy, the new Italian state was aided by the missionary work of the Roman Catholic Church. Although at loggerheads with each other because of the Roman Question, that is the military occupation of Rome and the Papal States, the presence of Italian missionaries in the 'frontier' areas of the world provided an opportunity for Italy to assess her chances of economic, political and military penetration in such areas.

Beside the African continent, Australia and the other lands of Oceania were among the places on which Italy cast her avid colonialist eyes. In fact Australia attracted the attention of Italian missionaries even before the Unification of Italy, indeed even before Captain James Cook claimed the east coast for Great Britain. Perhaps the first instance that bears witness of an Italian interest in this continent can be found in the map drawn in 1676, ninety-four years before Captain Cook's exploration of Australia's Eastern coast, by Father Vittorio Riccio, a Dominican missionary based in Manila. This map, prepared for the Congregation for the Propagation of the Faith in Rome, clearly shows Australia as a vast, accessible land mass or, in Riccio's words, 'Terra Australis, once unknown, now partly known'. He had drawn this map from information obtained from sailors and some natives from Terra Australis who had been brought to Manila on Dutch ships, which had possibly touched the shores of this great continent in the pursuit of trade and colonisation.

As was the case for Cristoforo Colombo and Amerigo Vespucci or for the scores of other lesser known Italian explorers who lent their services to other countries at the end of the eighteenth century, some Italians were also involved in the exploration of the Pacific as members of the Spanish or British Expeditions or as forced guests of His Majesty's ships bound for Botany Bay. Sometimes it is impossible and also historically irrelevant to prove that people with Italian-sounding names were indeed Italian. For instance, New York-born James Matra, of Corsican parents, who was with the First Fleet, could only remotely be considered Italian. The same could be said for Corsican-born Francois Rossi, who in 1825 became head of Sydney's police, or for the thousands of Italian-speaking Swiss who between 1830 and 1850 migrated to the colony of Victoria. More interesting is the case of Giuseppe Tusa, a First Fleeter deported to Botany Bay, who perhaps was a Spaniard or a Sicilian sailor drafted by the Royal Navy in Palermo, a supply port for the British fleet.

In March 1793, some time after the discovery of Australia, the Spanish vessels *Descubierta* and *Atrevida*, on a voyage of exploration around the world, berthed in Sydney. The expedition was led by Tuscan-born Alessandro Malaspina who, while in Botany Bay, carried out valuable scientific research, botanical surveys and astronomical

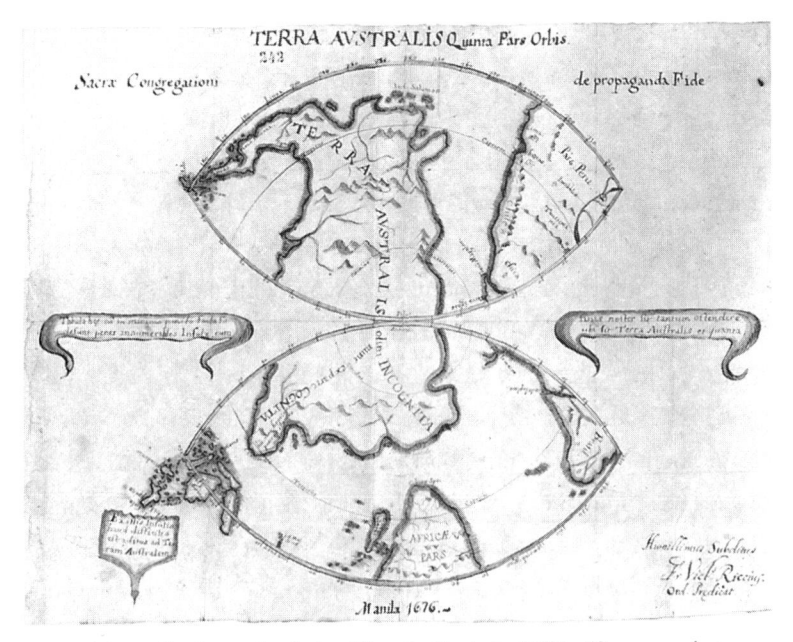

Map of Australia drawn by Father Vittorio Riccio in 1676. (Congregazione della Propaganda Fide Archives, Rome)

observations. Two Italian painters, Fernando Brambilla and Giovanni Ravenet, were also on board the ships. Brambilla painted some of the earliest landscapes of the colony including Parramatta; Ravenet sketched natives, convicts and free settlers.

Some Italians were also attached to British expeditions scouting the new Dominion. For instance, in February 1832 an Italian blacksmith, Stefano Bombelli, a member of the expedition to southern New South Wales organised by Thomas Livingstone Mitchell, who would become Surveyor-General of New South Wales, was murdered by the Aborigines together with one of his companions.

Italian missionaries were also most active in the exploration of Australia. Already in 1843 four Passionist priests, a Frenchman and three Italians, were brought to Sydney by John Bede Polding, the first Catholic Bishop in Australia. Their immediate impression of the colony was most enthusiastic. Father Raimondo Vaccari remarked that 'this fifth part of the world ... without the slightest exaggeration ... can be called a terrestrial paradise'. Later on, when they moved to Queensland and founded a mission for the Aborigines on Stradbroke Island, near Brisbane, they modified their opinion somewhat. Lack of water and the harsh living conditions met on this barren and inhospitable island compelled them to close the mission in 1845, whereupon they went to Adelaide to start a new one.

In 1845 another missionary, Angelo Confalonieri, arrived in Perth. Soon after he went to Port Essington (today's Darwin), where he worked among the Aborigines, learning their language, translating a small book of prayers and parts of the New Testament, compiling a dictionary of one of the Aboriginal languages and mapping the territory of the several tribes living on the Coburg Peninsula. When in 1848 he died after a short period of illness, the local military garrison buried him with full honours. In Western Australia, the New Norcia mission was set up in the late 1840s by the Spanish Benedictine Bishop Rosendo Salvado, aided by a group of twenty-seven missionaries among whom were two Italians, the already mentioned Angelo Confalonieri and Nicola Caporelli. They spread Christian values among the Aborigines of Western Australia and created the basis for future colonial settlements.

A further group of Italian missionaries arrived in Australia in the second half of the nineteenth century and established a network of religious assistance to the few hundred Italians then in this country, as well as to Australian Catholic parishioners, who were mainly of Irish extraction. Father Angelo Ambrosoli arrived in 1855 at the Benedictine monastery of Subiaco, Western Australia. In 1873 the Reverend Dr Antonini came to Queensland soon to be joined by Monsignor Fortini who went to Cooktown, in the far north. In

Some of Bishop Salvado's missionaries at work among Western Australian Aborigines in New Norcia, 1850s. (New Norcia Museum)

Stanthorpe, Queensland, Father Girolamo Davadi from the early 1870s earned the title of 'father of the fruit industry' for his agricultural activities. He brought from Italy knowledge of the culture of vineyards and of the making of wine. So great was his involvement in these activities that he must have neglected his spiritual duties, since Archbishop Dunne lamented that 'I hear of no movement towards doing anything for the interests of the Church'. Yet Davadi succeeded in erecting churches at Stanthorpe, Sugarloaf and Wallangarra.

The most important and charismatic figure among the Italian clergy in Australia was unquestionably 133 kilo Elzeario Torregiani,

Bishop of Armidale, who from 1879 until his death in 1904 administered the affairs of his huge diocese with wisdom and energy, opening fifteen schools, building many churches and increasing the number of priests from nine to nineteen.

The missionaries were soon followed by the emigrants, by the 'colonists'. Already in 1855 the Sardinian vessel *Goffredo Mameli* sailed from Genoa for Sydney with eighty-four emigrants on board. Its captain was Nino Bixio, Garibaldi's famous second-in-command, who on 16 December 1873 would die of yellow fever at Achin Bay in Sumatra, en route for Batavia, where he was directed to be in charge of a commercial expedition. The Sardinian Ministry of Foreign Affairs emphasised the importance of this voyage, hoping that 'in Australia our emigrants will enjoy a reputation of probity and disposition to work and that the future will bear evidence of this

Bishop Elzeario Torregiani of Armidale. (Diocesan Archives, Armidale)

truth'. Incidentally, Giuseppe Garibaldi himself in 1853 sailed the Victorian waters as captain of the *Carmen* and landed briefly at Three Hummock Island, in Bass Strait, to take on supplies of fresh water.

Although Garibaldi had only a fleeting encounter with Australia, his son, Ricciotti, came to live in Melbourne in 1874, where in 1879 he had a son, Giuseppe ('Peppino'), who would follow in the steps of his homonymous grandfather and fight for the independence of Greece, with the Boers in Traansval, in Mexico with Pancho Villa, and in Venezuela. During the First World War he commanded the Garibaldi Legion in France, where he was promoted to brigadier-general. He died in 1950.

It was nevertheless the discovery of gold that attracted most Italians to Victoria in the 1850s and to Western Australia in the 1890s. Before the Victorian gold findings and before the Unification of Italy in 1861, there were few Italians in Australia. But by mid-nineteenth century, emigration, adventurism and the seeking of political refuge inexorably drew people to escape from the Old World and its values to virgin lands where they had the chance of creating for themselves a new life and a new identity. Even Garibaldi, as he recalled in his *Autobiographical Memoirs*, later on in life felt the need to reflect with nostalgia upon his fleeting and idyllic encounter with the unspoiled underbelly of the Fifth Continent:

> How often has that lovely island in Bass Strait deliciously
> excited my imagination, when, sick of this civilised society,
> so well supplied with priests and police-agents, I returned in
> thought to that pleasant bay, where my first landing startled a
> fine covey of partridges, and where, amid lofty trees of a
> century's growth [was] the dearest, the most poetical of brooks,
> where we quenched our thirst with delight, and found an
> abundant supply of water for the voyage.

When news of the gold findings reached Europe by the early 1850s, scores of adventurers and migrants in search of quick fortune, among them several Italians, rushed to Melbourne, thus setting the basis for its rapid economic development. Mention of Italians at the goldfields is made in the few eyewitness accounts of those years, for instance in Carboni's *The Eureka Stockade*. The Polish Seweryn Korzelinski, in his *Memoirs of Gold Digging in Australia*, recollects that 'in the evenings we listened to the songs of the musical Italians'. Some towns like Daylesford had a population almost totally Italian, and some mines bore Italian names, like the Garibaldi claim, near Daylesford, sketched by the noted Swiss artist Eugene von Guerard. The foundation of a small Italian community on the Victorian goldfields resulted also in the establishment of small commercial

The Italian Stand at the Sydney International Exhibition of 1879.
(Mitchell Library, Sydney)

The old macaroni factory at Daylesford. (Mitchell Library, Sydney)

enterprises such as cafés, food factories and restaurants that aimed for the needs of the Italian migrant population. Typical of such enterprises was the old Macaroni factory, or the traditional Italian-style *pisé* and mudbrick houses, which still stand today at Daylesford.

Conditions on the goldfields were harsh and primitive. Many Italians soon found that they had pursued in vain their dream of quick fortune. Diplomatic despatches between the Kingdom of Sardinia and its representatives in Victoria make frequent reference to instances of destitute Italian miners at the goldfields in need of assistance. Frequently, migrants were a victim of swindles and malversation on the part of unscrupulous locals. In 1855 the Sardinian Consul-General in Sydney assured his superiors that he would give the newly arrived migrants 'directives and advice to guarantee them against the dangers and the deceptions which threaten usually the foreigners arriving in the colonies, to the profit of the most audacious speculators'.

Sometimes migrants joined their Australian 'mates' in their struggle to achieve better working conditions. In 1860 a group of Piedmontese stonemasons, employed ten hours a day on a railway project, went on strike in support of the eight-hour day. Two were arrested, brought before the Police Court and sentenced to short-term imprisonment. When they appealed, the Italian Consul General advised them against 'the futility of their action'.

New Italy settlers with grapes for winemaking, c. 1890. The first instance of Italian group settlement took place in 1885, when 217 survivors of a tragically failed attempt to form an Italian colony in an island of the Bismark Archipelago, near New Guinea, built a new village, New Italy, in northern New South Wales. The Italian immigrants, mainly from Friuli and the Veneto Region, recreated for themselves in Australia a lifestyle similar to the one they had left behind. New Italy had its own church, school, community hall, and organised debutantes' balls, cycling and bocce competitions. It sent silk artefacts to the Milan Trade Fair, where they won the First Prize in 1906. Growing grapes and making wine were also two of the main activities. Eventually the colonists intermarried with Australian youth, the drive and the enthusiasm of the earlier pioneering days were lost and the settlement was condemned to become yet another Australian ghost town. (Richmond River Historical Society Archives)

The oldest Italian settler of New Italy. (Mitchell Library, Sydney)

Yet political or industrial militancy on the part of Italian migrants was infrequent. They studiously kept a low profile. A report on the Italians at the goldfields, written in 1868 by the Consul-General in Melbourne, Giuseppe Biagi, stated that only 548 were registered at the Consulate-General, excluding those who had taken a Certificate of Naturalisation and those who had not bothered to register—and whom Biagi believed to be, only in Victoria, over 1000. 'The majority of Italians', remarked the Consul-General, 'are unaccounted for, because they are scattered throughout this colony. Most of them belong to the peasant and working classes and are employed at the goldfields or in the woods, cutting timber for the mines, and do not have a fixed address. Those who settle in country towns become farmers or manage hotels or small shops. Few are those who live in Melbourne, who are businessmen, and nobody has founded any Chamber of Commerce aiming at importing foods directly from our country'.

Most Italians, like everyone else on the goldfields, were adventurers in search of quick fortune. Among them was the noted Raffaello Carboni, actor in and witness and historian of the events which preceded and followed the bloody Eureka Stockade revolt in 1854. Other Italians were liberal and republican refugees of the revolutions of 1848, like the red-shirted Garibaldi's followers fossicking at Ballarat, according to Carboni's witness. One of the first political refugees to arrive was Count Girolamo Carandini, a Modenese liberal who escaped to Hobart in 1843, where he married the young singer Marie Burgess, whose family was connected with the poets Shelley and Byron. In 1845 they moved to Sydney, where a year later Carandini produced Verdi's revolutionary opera *Attila*. Another political refugee was Gian Carlo Asselin, a Neapolitan who had taken part in the liberal uprising of 1848 and in Garibaldi's unsuccessful attempt to wrest Rome from the Pope in 1849, and who would become Italian Vice-Consul in Sydney in 1861.

An Italian family in front of their home in the early days of the New Italy settlement. (Mitchell Library, Sydney)

Others still, arrived in later years, were successful entrepreneurs, like Angelo Bernacchi, who in 1884 started the industry of sericulture in Tasmania or, like Eugenio Vanzetti, who introduced new technologies in the mining industry in Western Australia. Or they were professional people, like architect Ugo Catani, designer of the Melbourne Botanic Gardens, or artists like painter Girolamo Nerli, or scientists like astronomer Pietro Baracchi. Or intelligent, skilled and imaginative people like Tommaso Fiaschi, a Florentine-born medical doctor who eloped with an Irish Catholic nun while they were both working at St Vincent's Hospital. After his elopement he was forced to resign and eventually worked at Sydney Hospital where he established a reputation as a brilliant surgeon. His interests extended to winemaking at his old home, 'Tizzana', on the Hawkesbury River near Windsor. A few were even convicts, like deportee No. 9161 Samuele Giorgetti from Viareggio, who landed in Fremantle in December 1866 to serve a ten-year sentence, one of the last people to be deported from England before the closure of the West Australian penal colony in 1867.

Before Unification, Italian entrepreneurs also tried, albeit unsuccessfully, to export industrial and commercial know-how to Australia. An interesting case in point was that of a Florentine business enterprise, manufacturer of mining equipment, Rogerius & Sons, which in 1853 made specific plans to send an expedition to the Australian goldfields to explore whether it was financially viable to set up locally a company with Tuscan capital, equipment and labour. Predictably, the project did not materialise.

Yet another indication of the greater relevance of Australia to Italians was the establishment in the mid-1850s of formal diplomatic relations between the Colonies of New South Wales and Victoria and the Kingdom of the Two Sicilies, the Grand Duchy of Tuscany and the Kingdom of Sardinia. Incidentally, the opening of the

Sardinian Consulate in Melbourne took place in grotesque circumstances. The Vice-Consul, Fabrizio Fabiani, who arrived in March 1856 on board the *Goffredo Mameli* to take charge of it, soon raised a storm of protest from the Italian community. A leading businessman, Bartolomeo Dardanelli, reported to the Sardinian Ministry for Foreign Affairs that Fabiani was living in a 'miserable hovel', unable to afford better accommodation and even pay for his board because he had 'not a cent in his pockets'; and had revealed himself to be 'lazy, good for nothing, capable of any venality and a true and unprincipled master of deceit'. Also, that the Vice-Consul had still to pay for his voyage on the *Goffredo Mameli*. Soon after, Fabiani, quite ingeniously, sold the office of Vice-Consul to a gullible English businessman and returned to Europe under the false name of L. Arena on board the *Kent*, upon releasing to its captain a promissory note, valid for life, to pay for the voyage.

The Unification of Italy in 1861 saw a dramatic shift in the interest for Australia by Italians. Whereas previously they had come to this country on their personal initiative, after 1861 the Italian Government began gathering up the threads of a policy of migratory, colonial and economic penetration in this region. After Unification, Australia was increasingly perceived as a land for emigrants, a commercial outlet where Italian foods could be sold, a market secured and an outpost set up for further colonial expansion.

In 1862 the issue of 'a special Italian colony in Queensland' was raised by the Italian Government with the Executive Council of that Colony. The Colonial Secretary, Robert Herbert, although favourable in principle to the idea, took pains to make it 'distinctly understood that immigrants from Italy should be principally of the labouring class, that is, agricultural labourers and shepherds. Immigrants from the higher and educated classes of society', went on the Colonial Secretary, 'are not likely to succeed in this Colony'. The formation of a special Italian colony did not take place. From 1862 onwards, Colonial and, later on, State and Federal governments would always discourage and obstruct the creation of separate enclaves of non-English-speaking population, because they were considered a threat to the homogeneity of Australian society.

In 1865 the Piedmontese Alessandro Martelli and the Tuscan Luigi Veroli established in Melbourne the Carrara Marble Works, which began importing marble artefacts and selling them throughout Australia with considerable success. The *Age* noticed that the marble, 'instead of being of the inferior sort which was usually exported to the colonies, was such as would be sent to London or Paris', while the *Herald* advertised the 'marble baths for those who are wealthy enough to indulge in such a luxury'.

Yet trade between the two countries remained very limited. Between 1855 and 1866 only a few Italian vessels arrived in Australia: the *Goffredo Mameli* in 1856 with a cargo of marble, bricks and wine from Genoa; the *Lidia* in 1859 with barley from Odessa and the *Amelia* in 1861 with sugar from Mauritius; the *Petronilla* and the *Aquila* in 1861 with cargo from China to Sydney, and the *Rosina* in 1866. This modest commercial presence obviously reflected the economic weakness which was even more paradoxically evident when compared with Italy's persistent and frustrating efforts to acquire colonial possessions in the Pacific and the Far East.

In fact, like every other respectable Great Power, not only did Italy send its warships to this region in an obvious exercise of gunboat diplomacy, but even contrived to achieve territorial gains vis-à-vis France, Germany and Great Britain. In June 1865 the corvette *Magenta* sailed for the Far East and visited Australia in 1867. During her stay, an exploration was made of Tasmania, which was documented in a book on the Tasmanian Aborigines, published in 1874, by Professor Enrico Hillyer Giglioli, a member of the expedition. The men-of-war *Vettor Pisani* and *Cristoforo Colombo* cruised in New Guinean and Australian waters in 1872 and 1878 respectively. In 1884 the corvette *Caracciolo* cast anchor in Sydney and Melbourne during its voyage around the world. In 1898 the cruiser *Etna* berthed in Sydney.

On the more factual level of colony grabbing, in 1869 the Italian Ministry of Foreign Affairs secretly financed an Italian adventurer, Emilio Cerruti, to organise an expeditionary corps in Singapore to take possession of the islands of Ke, An and Batchiane, near the New Guinean coast, after they had been purchased from the local 'indigenous chiefs'. The opposition of the Great Powers and Cerruti's failure to finalise the deal put an end to this venture in 1872. Concurrently, an attempt was made in 1870 to obtain land in Borneo for a penal colony, and an expedition under the command of Carlo Racchia sailed on the corvette *Principessa Clotilde*. Again, Italy's territorial aspirations were met with strong opposition by the United States, Great Britain and the Netherlands, and she was forced to relinquish her claim. Undaunted by these failures, in 1883 the Italian Government sounded out Great Britain about her reaction to an eventual Italian annexation of New Guinea. Lord Granville, the Foreign Secretary, pointed out to the Italian chargé d'affaires in London that this plan would clash with Australia's determination to resist foreign colonisation of the island. As a result, Italy abandoned her plans of gaining a colonial foothold in the Pacific.

Another course followed by Italy in the prosecution of her Great Power aspirations was that of taking part in foreign trade exhibitions such as the two International Exhibitions held in Sydney in 1879 and in Melbourne in 1888. In Melbourne Italy was represented by twenty-two companies promoting the typical Italian export commodities of those years: alabaster, statues, jewellery, Venetian glassware, furniture, wine, salami, pasta, paper, straw artefacts. Like her colonial pursuits, Italy's persistent efforts to increase her economic influence in the Pacific had limited and inconsequential success. Her main export to Australia remained people.

In the light of these unsuccessful imperial aspirations, the question of the establishment of Italian colonies in Australia acquires new meaning and a new historical dimension. In spite of Australian bureaucratic obstructionism, during the second half of the nineteenth century some important Italian settlements were formed in Queensland, New South Wales and Tasmania.

Again, it was the Catholic missionary hierarchy which, first and foremost, realised the need and the urgency to populate and exploit the empty spaces of the northern Australian frontier. In 1873 Bishop Quinn, who had experienced difficulties in securing Irish priests for the new colony of Queensland, went to Rome for assistance. Here he got his Irish priests, and at the same time induced a number of young middle-class Italians to emigrate down south. They were the first group of Italians to set foot in north Queensland, and many shared exceptional intellectual qualifications. Among them were the sculptor Achille Simonetti, the astronomer Canali, the musician Benvenuti, the educationist Papi, the botanist Richi, the businessmen Chiaffredo Venerano Fraire and Pio Vico Armati, and the already mentioned Reverend Dr Antonini.

In particular, it was after Italy and Great Britain signed a Treaty of Commerce and Navigation on 15 June 1883, which provided for their subjects to enter, travel, reside and acquire property in each other's colonial dominions, that Rome took a greater interest in Australia as a possible outlet for its emigrants.

On 12 April 1880, 240 people from the Veneto region were allowed to leave Italy to join an expedition organised by the Marquis De Rays, a Frenchman, to the island of New Ireland in the Bismarck Archipelago, where they arrived in October, on board the vessel

India. They were promised land, cheap labour, ready markets and a beautiful climate. None of these promises turned out to be true, and between November 1880 and March 1881, thirty-seven people died of malaria, dysentery and hunger. As a result of his swindle, the Marquis De Rays was jailed for criminal negligence. The survivors were brought to Sydney, where they arrived on 8 April 1881. In New South Wales they found hospitality and work with Australian families living in country areas.

Notice issued by the NSW Government upon the arrival in Sydney of the Italian survivors of the Marquis De Rays Expedition. (Cresciani Collection)

This solution was favoured by the government of Sir Henry Parkes, determined to avoid the concentration of Italians in a specific area. It was pointed out to the survivors that 'the customs of the country and other circumstances render it undesirable, indeed almost impossible, for them to settle down altogether in one locality'. Yet by 1885, forty families had gone to live at Woodburn, near Lismore, on 1226 hectares of land, where they built a village, the New Italy, a settlement which lasted until after the First World War.

Another important colony was founded at Maria Island, in Bass Strait. In 1884, Angelo Giulio Diego Bernacchi arrived in Hobart with his wife, Barbe, their three children and a nurse. He was a rich silk merchant from Lozza, near Como, in Lombardy. He arrived at Maria Island, formerly a penal settlement, to inspect its suitability for growing mulberry trees and producing silk. He was granted a lease of the island and by 1888 Darlington had been renamed San Diego and was a boom town with more than 250 residents who viewed Bernacchi as a benevolent employer. But the recession of the 1890s was to take its toll and in 1896 the Bernacchi family were forced to leave their beloved Maria Island to live in Melbourne. One year later they left for England with the younger children.

Yet another Italian enclave was allowed, this time indeed encouraged, to form in north Queensland in 1891. For over forty years the cane plantations of Queensland had been worked by the Kanakas. The Kanakas were indentured labour recruited, or often simply kidnapped, largely from the Solomon Islands, the New Hebrides and New Britain. This objectionable trade was known as 'blackbirding' and was a source of virtual slave labour. By the turn of the century, when the white Australia policy was established, public opinion had turned against this practice and the 17 000 Kanakas were sent back to their islands. Their repatriation left a vacuum which would be filled in part by Italian labour.

Blackbirding. (National Library of Australia)

Kanaka women at work on a sugar cane plantation. (John Oxley Library of Queensland)

Two Italians, Armati and Fraire, who had businesses in Townsville, were despatched to Italy—to Piedmont and Lombardy—to contract labourers, and the first batch of 335 arrived at Townsville in 1891, indentured by the Queensland Government. The Italians were paid about £1 a week and there seemed little chance of their rising above their role as labourers. But gradually, as family members followed each other to Australia, they began buying farms themselves. From 1891, when there were only 438 Italians in Queensland, their numbers grew to about 2000 by 1925. This was certainly not a great number but during that period they had managed to buy almost a third of the entire register of cane farms. Of about 150 plantations in Queensland, fifty-two were Italian-owned.

Yet not all migrants were peasants or miners. Some Italians brought to this country political infighting which had compelled them to leave their homeland. In the later part of the nineteenth century a group of about seventy anarchists and socialists, led by a brilliant and extrovert Sicilian intellectual, Francesco Sceusa, lived in Melbourne and Sydney. Many of them were cultured, idealist reformers, who struggled for the improvement in the social conditions of the migrant workers, such as Pietro Munari from Schio, Veneto, who wrote a very interesting book on Australia; Adalgiso Fiocchi, an anarchist from Milan, who taught Italian in Melbourne; newspaper editors Carlo Bentivoglio from Turin and Giuseppe Prampolini from Modena; and surgeons Quinto Ercole from Teramo and Divo De Marco from Camerino.

In Sydney they founded the Italian Workers' Welfare Society in aid of needy migrants, and carried out political activities against the Italian representatives in Australia. They also collected money for the victims of the Milan riots of 1898, when the Italian Army fired on a bread line, killing 200 people and injuring 1000, and for the diffusion of Socialist propaganda in Italy. They even stole official

Francesco Sceusa, c. 1874, when he was studying at the University of Naples. (Biblioteca Feltrinelli, Milan)

documents from the consular offices in Sydney and assaulted the Consul-General, Pasquale Corte. On 17 June 1882, Sceusa organised a memorial service for the death of Giuseppe Garibaldi at the Garden Palace in Sydney, attended by 10 000 people, and in 1893 he went to the International Socialist Congress at Zurich, Switzerland, to represent the Australian Workers' Movement.

In 1901 the group's activities were considered by the Italian authorities and by Interpol dangerous enough to alert the Australian Governor-General and the NSW Police Department about the possibility of terrorist acts being committed by such a group. The Italian Acting-Consul in Melbourne, L. Porena, went as far as warning Rome that 'the future of Italians in Australia is in the hands of these few malefactors', since political crimes eventually committed by them would undoubtedly result in 'the expulsion from Australia of all Italians'. Yet no crimes were ever committed, and no mass expulsion of Italians ever took place.

At the beginning of the twentieth century there were in Australia some 8000 Italians, although the 1901 census indicated that there were only 5678, the difference being made by those who did not bother to register and by the children born in Australia from Italian parents. The majority lived in the countryside, employed in agriculture, viticulture, railway building sites and mines. In the cities the range of their occupations varied considerably: in the main they were hotel keepers, painters, importers of foodstuffs, cooks and waiters, bakers, carpenters, tailors, labourers. There were few professional people, because their immigration was consistently discouraged by the Italian authorities who rightly saw that there was no chance for their employment in Australia. In 1899, Porena yet again warned that 'foreign professional people cannot find employment in these colonies; in fact, while some years ago two Italian architects were practising their profession in Victoria with moderate success, recently one was compelled to return to Italy and the other lives, almost forgotten, in a small township in the outback'.

Five generations of Italians at Gundagai, New South Wales, in the 1890s. (Mitchell Library, Sydney)

Notwithstanding the difficult economic conditions at the beginning of the century, Italians found in Australia a new outlet for migration, although, to the few Italians in Italy who had ever heard her name being mentioned, Australia was still, as it had been for Father Riccio 200 years before, a faraway 'Terra Australis, once unknown, now partly known'.

In the absence of an Italian political and military presence, without a direct shipping service from Italy, facing the opposition of the local authorities to a large influx of non-English-speaking people, frustrated by the exorbitant cost of the passage, not many Italians thought of Australia first as a choice for emigration. Yet some began to look at this new, mysterious and promising land. By 1900, a few had made up their minds and left the deprivation and ugliness of life in Italy to come to plague-threatened Sydney, or to the harsh conditions of the tropics, or to the equally primitive and destitute life of the Australian outback.

Theirs was a passage to another India. It was an escape from the subculture of the undeveloped, primitive, isolated, God-forsaken Italian south, colonised by ruthless northern bureaucrats and terrorised by the Piedmontese Army in its struggle against southern separatist banditry. It was also an unconscious, disappointing, and at times brutal reckoning with the reality of colonial Australia, with her prevailing subcultural cringe against foreigners, with the emerging hero-cult of the local brigands—the Ned Kellys, the bushrangers—with the isolation of the bush and the alienation of social discrimination.

If, for many of them, 'Christ had stopped at Eboli', as maintained by Italian writer Carlo Levi in his famous novel, if in Italy they had lived a primitive, almost animal-like existence, their new Australian experience was not much different. Indeed, for many 'wops', Christ had stopped also at Woop-Woop.

3
THE ITALIAN PRESENCE 1900–1940

At the turn of the century the movement towards federalism caught the imagination of Australia's 3.3 million people. After some fifty years of wrangles and disagreements, the colonies had finally agreed—and were permitted by Great Britain—to formally unite as federated states on 1 January 1901. In the climate of rhetorical nationalism which surrounded the event, the founding of the Commonwealth of Australia was proclaimed as the birth of 'a nation for a continent and a continent for a nation'. On the first day of the twentieth century a new chapter in Australia's history had begun.

The federation of the Australian colonies attracted the attention of the European Powers, among them the government of liberal Italy. At the turn of the century, the Italian Government was eager to increase Italian migration to Australia, because it constituted another *sbocco*, another outlet towards which to direct unemployed people who, if unable to emigrate, would have worsened what was undoubtedly Italy's gravest social question. In order to forestall this emerging crisis, a Commissariat-General for Emigration was created in 1901, with the task of overseeing Italian emigration and affording legal protection to the migrants, once settled abroad. Anxious to increase the pace of this enormous drain of human resources, the

An anti-Italian cartoon. (Western Mail, 1904)

Italian Commissar-General for Emigration declared in 1906 that 'we must prepare new outlets for our emigration, also in view of possible restrictions upon our migration towards the Americas and especially the United States'. America would severely limit immigration in 1921.

Unavoidably, the issue of emigration at this time was inextricably linked with the policy of colonial and imperial expansionism then pursued by the Italian Government. Italy, notwithstanding repeated rebuffs, still believed that it was possible to create abroad colonial enclaves of Italian migrants who would enhance her international prestige. Nationalist propaganda dictated that it was Italy's 'sacred duty', or, to adapt Rudyard Kipling's immortal phrase, that it was the New Italian man's burden, to maintain and to rekindle periodically the patriotism of overseas Italians. To this purpose, in 1905, Rome sent the cruiser *Calabria* to visit Australian ports, in a typical exercise of gunboat diplomacy.

So Italy's poor who, until Federation, had come to Australia in their hundreds, now began arriving by the thousands. Ahead, for most of them, lay a life of rejection, discrimination, hardship and even violence. Many had endured a long voyage, often under appalling conditions. Italian writer Edmondo De Amicis was deeply shocked when he witnessed the inhuman treatment, already referred to, that was meted out to migrants by unscrupulous and greedy shipping companies. In his book *On The Ocean* he condemned

> the appalling conditions [that] existed under deck, in the large dormitory ... by looking down into it, one could see in the semi-darkness bodies piled over bodies ... and therefrom, as from an underground hospital, a concert of laments, of gasps, of coughs was coming up, making the listener feel like disembarking at the first port of call ... The stench was unbearable, considering that it was coming from human beings, and it was frightening to think what could have happened if an infectious disease would have spread on board.

Italians in a mine shaft at Walhalla, Victoria, 1907. (Bollettino dell'Emigrazione, Rome)

However, Italians continued to arrive in Australia in increasing numbers, although figures on Italian immigration during the period 1901–21 show that the Italian presence in this continent was and remained very modest indeed, if compared with emigration to the Americas. The census of 1901 indicated that there were 5678 Italians in Australia, distributed as follows:

State	Males	Females	Total
New South Wales	1243	334	1577
Victoria	1289	236	1525
Queensland	708	137	845
South Australia	293	34	327
West Australia	1296	58	1354
Tasmania	42	8	50

These figures are not accurate, since many migrants scattered in the outback or, unaware of the census, did not register. A report written in 1910 claimed that well over 1000 Italians had not been accounted for, and if to this number are added the 500 children born of Italian parents, it can be safely assumed that the number of Italians in 1901 was approximately 7000. The 1921 census revealed that there were 8135 Italians in Australia, although, for the same reasons, this figure is not accurate either. In fact the Italian Commissariat-General for Emigration estimated that at that time the number was approximately 15 000.

During the first four decades of nationhood, Australia came face to face with the differences existing between the two Italies, the two cultures, the two societies represented by the vastly different kinds of Italians who had landed on her shores. One was the small, mostly invisible nucleus of educated middle-class Italians—those who came to Australia as consular representatives, as traders and businessmen, executives of shipping companies or just as visiting celebrities.

The other society comprised the overwhelming majority of migrants: destitute peasants, illiterate or semi-literate, who would at best be neglected and forgotten by the governments of liberal as well as Fascist Italy. These people migrated to escape the shackles of their centuries-old conditions. They brought with them their apathy towards authority, their suspicion for the educated, their hatred of poverty. In Australia they found themselves estranged from the Australian community and from the Italian Establishment in exactly the same way as in their villages at home they were alienated from the *Signori*, the *Baroni*, the *Dottori*.

Yet the ones who were successful in landing in Australia could consider themselves lucky—lucky because, although destitute and illiterate, they had been accepted against legislative and social odds. In fact barriers against Italian emigration to Australia were set up almost immediately after Federation. The Immigration Restriction Act No. 17 of 1901 not only prevented the landing in Australia of people who were illiterate, but also of people who had obtained a work contract from an Australian employer. This measure was aimed at protecting the Australian workforce to the disadvantage of the newcomers. 'The Australian government', commented the Italian Ministry of Foreign Affairs, 'wants to avoid the coming of migrants to the Commonwealth with the certainty of finding a job with a work contract. Migrants must go to Australia only with the hope of finding employment, and under those conditions which will be offered to them at their arrival.'

In fact the labour movement and the Labor Party were hostile to the settlement of migrants, especially if non-English-speaking, because the latter were introducing a new undesirable element of competition into the already highly competitive labour market. The accusation was frequently levelled against migrants that they were meekly accepting lower wages and worse working conditions than their Australian counterparts, thus endangering the benefits and

Italian workers standing on felled timber, c. 1908. (Bollettino dell'Emigrazione, Rome)

achievements gained by Australian workers after many years of struggle with their employers. This, unfortunately, was often the case. In 1900 Consul-General Pasquale Corte warned the Italian Government that Italian workers should not be allowed to migrate to Australia because of an outbreak of bubonic plague and because of the great number of unemployed miners who had come to Australia from the Transvaal. In 1904 a wave of anti-Italian feeling broke out in Western Australia, where the Press and the Labor Party accused Italians of being 'scabs'. In North Queensland in the same year, when some farmers sought Italian labourers to take the place of the repatriated Kanakas, the local Labor members of Parliament wrote to their comrades of the Italian Socialist Party urging them to do everything possible to discourage further migration to that State. Anti-Italian feelings emerged again in 1906, when Italy began negotiating with the Government of Western Australia to establish migrant enclaves there. A party of three Italian specialists arrived and reported favourably on the conditions which migrants would encounter. There was a general outcry. After two years of negotiations the project was abandoned due to public opposition on the grounds that the settlements would be simply too 'Italian' in character.

Misunderstanding and bigotry were ever present, even at the highest levels. In 1904 King O'Malley, who in 1913 would lay the foundation stone of Canberra, alleged that Italians 'walk with a razor in their jacket and a knife in their boots'. Even responsible leaders of the labour movement like William Lane, William Spence and the first Labor Prime Minister, John Watson, were openly racist in their attitudes and were instrumental in introducing and enacting the odious Immigration Restriction Act and the language dictation test, given in a foreign language unknown to the person examined, which effectively barred entry to Australia and allowed the deportation of anybody classed as undesirable.

Some influential sections of the Australian Press also showed a discernible bias against migrants. Already in 1893, the *Bulletin* maligned the Italian migrant 'with his stiletto and his dirt and his vast and wonderful ignorance'. The newspaper which distinguished itself for its rambling xenophobia and unfounded accusations was undoubtedly *Smith's Weekly*. For years its pages were filled with vicious anti-Italian propaganda, a fair example being the slur printed in 1926 that Italians were a 'dirty Dago pest' and 'that greasy flood of Mediterranean scum that seeks to defile and debase Australia'.

The accusation of Italians selling their labour cheaply, of being scabs, was perhaps the most consistent slur, and two Royal Commissions, one in Western Australia in 1904 and the other in Queensland in 1925, were set up to inquire into the reasons behind the widespread anti-Italian feeling so prevalent among the local residents. It is important to understand the demoralising effect that this climate of unfriendliness had on Italian migrants, because, together with geographic isolation and the insufficient protection afforded them by the Italian diplomatic representatives, it was one of the factors that determined their attitudes towards Italy as well as towards their country of adoption. In fact it is hardly surprising that many Italian migrants shunned social contacts with the Australian community and took a defensive posture in their 'little Italies'. They worked, built their homes, associations and clubs, founded newspapers and took scant interest in the affairs of their Fatherland, or, for that matter, of their country of adoption. To them, withdrawn in the security of their homes and clans, this behaviour represented a historically well-tested, inbuilt mechanism of defence and survival. Indeed, this was the very attitude which was objectionable to many Australians who deplored the Italians' failure to 'assimilate'.

By 1900, a strong reason to make Australia attractive to some Italian migrants was, yet again, the discovery of gold, this time in Western Australia. Italians flocked to the mines at Broad Arrow, Southern Cross, Day Down, Lennonville, Cue, Bulong, Kalgoorlie, Leonora, Laverton, Kanowna, Boulder and Wiluna. On the goldfields they found employment mainly as miners, woodcutters, labourers, foodstore owners, cooks and waiters. Working conditions were harsh. At the Great Fingall Mine (Day Down) during the years 1897–98 alone, more than seventy Italian miners died by poisoning from gunpowder fumes.

Elsewhere, migrants were employed in several other occupations. Piedmontese, Lombards and Tuscans found work in agriculture, viticulture, on railway building sites or as hotel-keepers; Sicilians in the fruit and fish industry; Friulians and people from the Veneto as terrazzo workers; Aeolian Islanders as fruit and vegetable growers and marketers; Neapolitans and people from Lucania as barbers, travelling salesmen, cobblers, shoemakers, florists and organ-grinders.

THE ITALIAN PRESENCE 59

Italian miners in a pit at Broken Hill. Following the discovery in September 1883 of huge iron, silver and lead deposits in Broken Hill, New South Wales, migrants from many nations, among them Italians, converged on this centre in the outback in search of fortune. By 1889, 20 000 people were struggling for quick and easy money in the mining pits of Broken Hill, which soon became one of the strongholds of Australian trade unionism. Italians were a significant and vocal component of the Amalgamated Miners' Association, which was defending miners' rights. In 1891, Broken Hill witnessed a bitter four-month strike, following the revocation of an industrial agreement by the Broken Hill Proprietary Company Limited. The dispute ended with the victory of the company and the significant weakening of the trade union movement. (Cresciani Collection)

The last, complained the Italian Consul of Perth, 'are here, as elsewhere, the plague of our emigration, and it would be a good thing to lose even the memory of them'.

Notwithstanding the harsh environment, the different religious, cultural and social habits, the diffidence if not the open hostility of the Anglo-Saxon majority, most of the few thousand Italians who had settled in Australia had, economically speaking, done very well for themselves. These observations were made in 1908 by an Italian missionary, Giuseppe Capra, who toured all the Australian States and reported back to Rome on the bright future that faced prospective migrants.

Yet a closer examination of the established pattern of Italian settlement in Australia reveals the peculiar and recurrent phenomenon of social and cultural isolation paradoxically mixed with economic success. An extremely interesting report written in 1911 by Capra claimed that many Italians in Australia were illiterate, and could not and did not write to their families in Italy unless they found someone who could write for them, and that was not easy. Their isolation from Italy was increased by the fact that they could not read the Italian Press or the few Italian books available. The small Italian library in Melbourne, for instance, in 1910 lent one book only, and not to an Italian.

Accustomed to a life of isolation and deprivation, many migrants were hostile to any effort made by the *signori* to improve their conditions. When, in 1908, an attempt was made to set up a school for the Italian fishermen of Fremantle, all illiterate, the fishermen wanted nothing to do with it; similarly, an Italian school had opened in Sydney a few years before but had to close for lack of community support. In 1897 Consul-General Corte had tried unsuccessfully to organise branches of the Dante Alighieri Society in Sydney and Melbourne. Even the *Società di mutuo soccorso* (Welfare Society), aiming at helping needy Italians, attracted little interest: in 1902 Italian welfare societies were opened in Melbourne, Sydney, Brisbane and Fremantle, but the Sydney society soon ceased to exist for lack of members, and Melbourne's had only thirteen or fourteen members. Social clubs suffered the same fate. In 1909 there were in Australia only two clubs, both in Sydney: the Circolo Isole Eolie, founded in

Kalgoorlie Riots, 1934. A hotel was wrecked during riots against Italian and Slav migrants (West Australian)

1903, and the Società Stella d'Italia—both without fixed premises, their main activity being the celebration of the *Festa dello Statuto* (Constitution Day) and of the anniversary of Italy's annexation of Rome on 20 September 1870. Attempts at forming social clubs at Kalgoorlie and Lismore (NSW) also failed.

Besides, the presence of the Italian authorities was quite inadequate. The Consulate-General in Melbourne faced the impossible task of having to assist its subjects in Australia without the backing of any other consulate. And, unlike the situation in other countries, there was no official of the Commissariat-General for Emigration stationed in Australia to listen to the grievances of the migrants and protect their interests. Thus it is hardly surprising that, as Father Capra noted in 1911, 'there is almost no direct contact between the consul and Italian migrants, with the exception of infrequent, unavoidable business dealings'. Absent from Australia were Italian welfare organisations working among migrants abroad, such as the Socialist Società Umanitaria or the Catholic Opera

Bonomelli, and there were no political contacts between Italian migrants and Italian and Australian political parties. Even migrants who had been militant in Italy and who worked in Sydney and in the mining centres shunned contacts with Australian political parties because of their xenophobic attitudes.

Before the First World War, most migrants were completely cut off from the events taking place in Italy, nor did they care much about them. Quite appropriately, Father Capra remarked that 'by not reading, not having access to newspapers, books, nor contacts with the Homeland, by never going back home, by not talking about Her, migrants tend to ignore Her, when they do not forget Her completely'. Yet to the very few who could read and who took an interest in Italian affairs, the Italian Press in Australia was a very rich source of information. In July 1903 there appeared in Sydney the newspaper, *Uniamoci* (Let's unite). Its editor was Giuseppe Prampolini, a revolutionary socialist who would play an important role in the history of the Italian labour movement after his return to Italy in 1904. This weekly tried to convince Italian migrants of the necessity for a concerted effort in order to combat apathy, hostility and economic hardships, albeit unsuccessfully. Prampolini admitted in the last issue (17 August 1904), that 'our mission was not completely successful, not for any fault of ours, but because of the social environment, in the main refractory to everything that is not personal interest'.

Uniamoci was followed in 1905 by the *Italo-Australiano*, which ceased publication in 1909, and by *Oceania*, which appeared on 12 July 1913 and lasted until 13 February 1915. Both newspapers were owned by and advocated the interests of the Italian Establishment in Australia and of the business elite, and therefore were largely unrepresentative of the interests and the opinions of the majority of illiterate, working-class and peasant migrants.

Italian migrants in Australia were nonplussed by the constant stream of patriotic propaganda printed by the Italian newspapers or uttered by their owners. They could not even read it, let alone understand it. They were more impressed and concerned by the simple facts of life, by those things which affected them most. For instance, they were surprised, as was one peasant who came to Western Australia, by the fact that 'here it is not allowed to spit on the footpath, and heavens forbid if someone sees you with a button of your trousers out of place'. They were confused and embittered when, as happened in Broken Hill, they were invited by the management of the mines to work in place of striking Australian workers,

Prampolini's newspaper Uniamoci, *which appeared in Sydney in 1903–4*
(Mitchell Library, Sydney)

Official opening of the Cavour Club in Melbourne, 1918. (Italian Historical Society, Melbourne)

only to be manhandled by the latter and compelled to leave town. They could not see how impassioned haranguing on the greatness of the Fatherland, on the glory that Italy would be, could help them in their daily struggle for life. It was incongruous to pretend, as the Italian Press in Australia did, that they could become involved in the process of national resurgence, to ask 'proletarian Italy' to awake. In their experience, liberal Italy (as later on, though to a lesser extent, Fascist Italy and republican Italy) was a distant and lost country, to look back to with nostalgia, perhaps, but with little regret for the life they had left behind.

The outbreak of the First World War put a temporary end to the flow of Italian migrants to Australia. By April 1915, with the signing of the secret Treaty of London, Italy and Australia had become allies in the Great War, and as a result thousands of migrants were returned to their Fatherland, in many cases forcibly, to serve under the colours. Conversely, after 1918 Australian soldiers returned from the conflict to a heroes' welcome and the prospect of unemployment. The government responded with retraining schemes and also established the Murrumbidgee Irrigation Scheme, aimed at developing desert lands around Griffith, New South Wales, to which ex-servicemen flocked to take up grants in what would become Australia's largest block of intensive farming land. Unfortunately these men were often devoid of any farming experience and during the 1920s and 1930s a steady influx of Italian migrants slowly took over the many farms which had proved unproductive in the hands of their Australian owners. At first they had worked in gangs, digging the irrigation channels or as labourers. Later they invested their savings in buying land. With a background of small-acreage farming, with hard work and agricultural skill, the Italian population of Griffith rose from thirty-three in 1921 to the extent that by 1940 Italians owned 23 per cent of all the farms, and by 1954 nearly half of them.

Building an irrigation channel in the Murrumbidgee Irrigation Area. (Water Resources Commission, Sydney)

Also immediately after the First World War, as in previous periods of social unrest and economic depression, episodes of intolerance and violence against migrants took place. Unquestionably, Italian labour in the canefields of North Queensland, in the mines of Western Australia and in the fields of the Murrumbidgee Irrigation Area was competing with Australian labour for the few jobs available. This situation worsened the already strained relations between the migrants and the Australian workforce.

On 12 August 1919, in Kalgoorlie, following a brawl between Italian and Australian patrons at the Café Majestic, an Australian war veteran was fatally wounded. Four Italians were immediately arrested by the police, and one of them was charged. A few hours later a crowd of hundreds of returned soldiers, marching behind the Union Jack, began assaulting Italians in the streets. The Glen Devon Hotel and the All Nations Hotel, frequented mainly by Italians, as well as shops and property owned by Italians, were ransacked and destroyed. Indeed, anti-Italian feeling was running high, judging

The family of Antonio Bugno, the first Italian settlers in the Murrumbidgee Irrigation Area, c. 1926. (Cresciani Collection)

from the countless petitions received by the Federal Government urging the deportation of aliens or at the very least preferential treatment for Australian labour.

In 1925, the increasing success of Italian farmers in the canefields of northern Queensland provoked resentment and tension. In particular, the Australian Workers' Union was concerned for its members' jobs, considered to be threatened by the spreading of Italian family-owned businesses. The Union pressured the Queensland Government into staging an inquiry. The resulting report became known as the Ferry Report, from the name of its Commissioner, Thomas A. Ferry, but its official title was the 'Inquiry into and the Report on the Social and Economic Effects of the Increase in the Number of Aliens in North Queensland'. The report, though at times racist and biased, was a vindication of the Italians. It stated that they were most acceptable in terms of commercial viability, standard of living, adherence to union rules and respect for social conventions.

In 1929, primary producers were the first to be hit in Australia by the Wall Street crash and the world economic crisis. The next five years would see Australia's economy in chaos. Any business that managed to survive could not make a profit. Bankruptcy was endemic and the currency was devalued by 25 per cent. Nearly a third of the workforce was unemployed. In fact the Great Depression hit hardest the most disadvantaged group in society. Many Italian migrants were compelled to move from job to job, from state to state, in order to survive. A case indicative of the mobility of the Italian migrants' workforce at the time is that of a peasant from the Veneto region who, between 1932 and 1939, survived by working as club secretary and newspaper editor in Melbourne, canecutter in Ingham, tobacco grower in Stanthorpe, vegetable grower in St Ives in outer Sydney, clothing seller in Western Australia, fruit picker in

Griffith, pie seller in Melbourne, tomato grower in Smithfield, and a number of other jobs. In 1930, again in Queensland, the Australian Workers' Union and Employer Associations came to an agreement effectively to ban Italian labourers from the canefields. As the Union paper, *The Worker*, stated, 'they were of an inferior type, and were a direct menace to our standard of living'. The British Preference League for Anglo-Celtic workers came into being in result of this 'Gentleman's Agreement'.

It was within this context of social and economic competitiveness that one of the most serious cases of racial violence in Australia's history took place in January 1934, again in Kalgoorlie. Here, as in other mines in Western Australia, resentment against Italian labour ran high because, as a report stated, Italians 'had the virtue of competitive docility and temperance and the ability to work in the hottest weather; consequently they were sought after by contractors'. Following a fight at one of the city pubs between its Italian owner and an Australian patron who was accidentally killed, a witch-hunt of Italian and Slav migrants swept through the town and surrounding district. During the riots, five hotels, four clubs, two boarding houses, eight cafés and fish shops, forty-nine houses and sixty-eight camps were smashed, looted and set ablaze. Three people were killed and scores of people received gunshot wounds. When it was over the Italians left the city, never to return.

Despite the general climate of suspicion, and even open hostility and social hatred towards the Italians, during this period there also took place in Australia amazing episodes of admiration and adulation for Italian personalities. There was an apparent ambiguity in public opinion about Italians. Visiting celebrities might get public adoration, but such events did not affect the attitude of the average Australian, who often saw 'dagoes' as a lesser breed of human. Perhaps the reason for this ambiguity was that Australians preferred to ignore the fact that they also had once been migrants and now were subconsciously choosing to identify with glory and success, even if foreign, and to shun the poverty and struggle that reminded them so much of their early and harsher days.

Thus there were wild scenes and enthusiastic tributes to an Italian flyer and his flight assistant when they arrived from Rome in a twin-engined seaplane in 1925. Wing Commander Francesco De Pinedo's exploit was one of many aimed at gaining international prestige for Fascist Italy. De Pinedo later became Chief of the Italian Airforce. Thousands of people lined the foreshores wherever the seaplane landed and the two Italians were fêted at endless public receptions during their stay. At one of these receptions, Prime Minister Stanley Bruce went as far as saying it was regrettable that the two aviators should be expected to speak in English: 'It is yet

Wing Commander De Pinedo arrives in Sydney, 1925. (Italo-Australian)

another instance of our disgusting insularity. We should take pride in understanding them in Italian'. He went on to say, 'We love Italy, we like the Italians and we welcome them'. From this comment one would be tempted to surmise that Australia, as well as Italy, was inhabited by two vastly different societies, constituted of Australians who had opposing perceptions of Italian migrants.

Australians had always exhibited a love for Italian opera and music. When Italian soprano Toti Dal Monte married her leading tenor, Enzo De Muro Lomanto, in St Mary's Cathedral in Sydney in 1928, a crowd estimated at 25 000 surrounded the cathedral. Sydney had never enjoyed a more spectacular wedding, claimed the *Sydney Morning Herald*.

Yet it is difficult not to remain perplexed when faced by this apparent ambiguity in the pattern of behaviour by Australian public opinion. The fact is that the exciting but fleeting experience of De Pinedo's courage, of Dal Monte's voice, were not deeply affecting the life of the man in the street. The Italian migrant, on the other hand, who had no myth, no charisma behind which to shield himself, was perceived by, and indeed represented to, the average Australian as an immediate potential danger to his standard of living. He was a threat too, because he was bringing to this country the seeds of different traditions, customs and culture or, to put it in Commissioner Ferry's exquisitely racist words, 'an undigested mass of alien thought, alien sympathy and alien purpose'.

Migrants, quite unrealistically, were expected to cast away overnight their personal experiences, memories, cultural background, religious beliefs and even their language, and were solicited willingly to undergo that doubtful, demoralising and dastardly exercise of psychological emasculation called assimilation. They were objected to not only because they were competing for the few jobs available, or because they were unwilling to conform to the Australian way of

Toti Dal Monte and Enzo de Muro Lomanto at their wedding in St Mary's Cathredral Sydney, 1928. (Italo-Australian)

life (whatever that meant), or because they looked 'different' and had customs and habits which were 'strange'. By 1939 they were also widely considered to be a potential threat to the security of Australia, a fifth column within the nation, under the mistaken assumption that being Italian automatically meant being a Fascist.

Yet notwithstanding shameful instances of xenophobia, intensified in the 1920s and 1930s by ignorance, by the Depression and by the issue of Fascism, Italians in Australia preferred to remain in this country, largely because of the economic security they had attained and the opportunities that had always been and still were unattainable in their place of origin. Indeed, like the proverbial soldiers of a defeated army, they had voted with their feet, choosing between the alienation of poverty in Italy and the alienation of what Prampolini had called 'the personal interest' in Australia. To this extent, they had successfully become 'assimilated' to what some of us still eagerly call 'the Australian way of life'.

4
FASCISM AND ANTI-FASCISM 1922–1940

At the end of the First World War Italy was left, like other victorious as well as defeated European powers, with a legacy of destruction, social dislocation, economic depression and political upheaval. The war had been fought by an army formed to a large extent by peasant draftees from the underdeveloped regions of the north and of the south; that is, by those very people who before the Great War had been migrating *en masse* to the Americas to escape malaria, poverty, hunger and exploitation.

Their losses had been high, over 600 000 dead, over 1 million injured. Yet the conflict had been a revelation to these deprived people who traditionally had been kept to the margins of mainstream Italian history. The millions of southern peasant soldiers, drafted and transported north, to the frontline or to defend cities, villages and industries, became aware, for the first time, of the existence of a world vastly different from their own, of a social, political and economic reality which forced them to question the humanity and the justice of their timeless condition of poverty, inequality and oppression. For the first time they experienced and became involved in trade unions and party-organised political activities. Demonstrations against the war, against shortages and restrictions, against the government, against their being aimlessly butchered in the trenches of the Carso, were savagely suppressed by the authorities. In Turin, the army put down the bread riots which took place in summer of 1917 by firing on the crowd and killing forty-one people—a repeat of what had happened in Milan in 1898.

Unlike other industrialised countries, Italy's economic and financial structure and its ruling class could not and would not meet the rising expectations of the organised masses. During the war people had been promised land ownership and social reforms. At the end of the conflict, encouraged by the political apprenticeship served in the armed forces and back at their god-forsaken, desolate villages of the north or in the extensive landed estates of the south, they demanded to be given what they had been promised. Peasant strikes, occupation of the land and the factories, foundation of leagues, unions, co-operatives and political organisations took place everywhere across the Italian peninsula, adding to the economic upheaval caused by the war.

Street riots, Rome, 1921. Police and demonstrators clash near the Coliseum. (Istituto Luce, Rome)

While the National Government witnessed impotently the unfolding of these events, landowners and industrialists supported, financed and armed whoever was opposed to the popular awakening. In this way they exploited the rising fear of revolution, the general discontent and the widespread disillusionment that followed the war years, years remembered with nostalgia by many returned soldiers as the period in which they had 'lived dangerously' and heroically. Nationalist rhetoric conditioned the behaviour of people, polarised ideas and fanned hatred of political opponents. The glorious days of the world conflict, seen by many as the time when they had been the participants in momentous historical events, were gone. Now, Socialism, Catholicism and Democracy were identified as the debasing, anti-national treacherous ideologies that were undermining national morale and that had to be fought and destroyed at all costs.

Out of this dramatic historical context Fascism was born. It was a movement of reaction against demands made by the Socialist and Catholic masses to change the social, economic and political status quo of the nation in favour of the underprivileged classes. Its supporters, organised in paramilitary squads called *squadre d'azione*, were members of the lower middle class who felt threatened by the social demands and political claims of the rising working class and the peasantry. Landowners and industrialists financed them, and the police and army aided and abetted them, even supplying them with weapons and ammunition. Between 1919 and 1922, with the connivance of successive Liberal governments which tried unsuccessfully to ride the Fascist tiger, the Fascist squads waged a bloody civil war against their opponents. These governments, which shared with the Italian Establishment and the Church a deep concern about the ominous threat represented by the Bolshevik Revolution and about the spread of its infectious message of liberation, allowed Fascism to terrorise, repress, burn and kill systematically. After three years

On 13 July, 1920 in Trieste, Fascist squads, led by Francesco Giunta, who in 1923 would become General Secretary of the Fascist Party, attacked and burned down the Narodni Dom (House of the People), headquarters of Slav nationalist organisations. This was the first large-scale Fascist action against its opponents. Police and Carabinieri did not intervene, but assisted in the criminal assault. One person was killed and several injured. (Cresciani Collection)

of street violence, social collapse and political chaos, in October 1922 Victor Emmanuel III—the 'soldier King' as he enjoyed being addressed—called petit-bourgeois *cavaliere* Mussolini to power in a *coup d'état*.

The successful Fascist bid for power culminated in the so-called March on Rome when a few thousand members of the Fascist squads—formed by idealists as well as the thugs and criminals who had terrorised their political opponents with the connivance of the authorities—were brought to Rome by special trains and paraded in front of the King and the new Prime Minister—the former migrant schoolteacher, journalist, renegade socialist and future Duce of Fascism Benito Mussolini.

After 1922 Fascism transformed itself from a political movement with radical, even leftist tendencies into a regime, although it never achieved such totalitarian control of Italian society as did Hitler in Germany or Stalin in the Soviet Union. Mussolini was unable and perhaps unwilling to carry out a social revolution, to destroy the Liberal structure of power, to eliminate the Liberal Establishment. Instead, a compromise was tacitly agreed on whereby Il Duce could speak of a Fascist revolution, well knowing that this was empty rhetoric, while the Liberal Establishment traded the limited democratic freedoms gained during the Risorgimento for the concession of being allowed to maintain its privileged position of economic power and political influence.

The march on Rome. A Fascist column enters Piazza del Popolo, 29 October 1922. (Archivio Centrale dello Stato, Rome)

Violence would be used by the Fascist State only against its uncompromising and indomitable opponents, who would be jailed, forced into exile or even callously murdered, like the priest Don Minzoni, the intellectual Piero Gobetti, the Socialist leader Giacomo Matteotti, the Liberal politician Giovanni Amendola. The defeat of liberalism, of democracy as it was then known in Italy, meant primarily the defeat of the aspirations of workers and peasants, who would from now on turn again to emigration as their only hope of achieving liberation from their centuries-old condition of social and economic exploitation.

Since migration to the United States had been severely restricted by the imposition on 19 May 1921 of the quota system, emigration to alternative countries increased significantly. Between 1922 and 1930, some 25 000 people left Italy for Australia, whereas before there were only approximately 8000 Italians in this country. Some

An anti-Fascist 'subversive' being arrested by the Carabinieri, Italy's Military Police. (Istituto Luce, Rome)

FASCISM AND ANTI-FASCISM

Anti-Fascist leader Omero Schiassi, in the uniform of Officer of the Italian Alpini Corps, c. 1915. (Cresciani Collection)

Dissident Fascist Franco Battistessa, 1927. (Cresciani Collection)

of these newcomers to Australia were not just traditional migrants, but people who had seen the birth of Fascism in Italy and were militantly opposed to it, who had been persecuted for their ideals and compelled to emigrate after it came to power. These Italians were predominantly industrial and agricultural workers from the northern part of the country and from the Po river valley. Unavoidably, the political infighting and the violence which marred Italy before the advent of Fascism were brought to this country by the new wave of emigrants.

Once in Australia, anti-Fascist Italians preferred to settle in areas where there was already a high concentration of their countrymen: in the sugar fields of northern Queensland, in the cities of Sydney and Melbourne, in the industrial and mineral centres of Corrimal, Wonthaggi, Lithgow, Broken Hill, Kalgoorlie, Boulder, Wiluna, and in the agricultural areas of Griffith and Lismore. Their presence in the midst of communities which also harboured pro-Fascist elements sparked frequent clashes. In the cities, they lived in boarding houses, where after a day's work they met, played cards and *bocce* (Italian bowls) and discussed politics. On the whole, they preferred to congregate with people of the same village and region. Moreover, new immigrants brought into the boarding houses the latest news from Italy, about the native village, the economic conditions that had compelled them to emigrate, the political situation and the determination of Fascism to make life difficult for the opposition.

These first-hand, emotional reports had a strong impact on the boarders, who were in the main young, single and class-conscious, and in this respect the boarding houses performed the function of centres of anti-Fascist political indoctrination and propaganda. Although holding different political beliefs, the Italian Republicans, Socialists, Communists and Anarchists in Australia had in common their hatred for Fascism. The political climate was so tense in areas of northern Queensland that Fascists were compelled to leave the area, to the extent that the pro-Fascist Italian newspaper *Italo-Australian* lamented in 1925 that 'the fact is that almost all Italians in north Queensland are bitter and irreconcilable enemies of Fascism'. It was in north Queensland, in March 1925, that there occurred the first anti-Fascist demonstration in Australia. When three Fascists from Mantua, who had been involved in beatings of anti-Fascists, arrived in Halifax they were confronted by other anti-Fascists, assaulted and forced to drink castor oil.

Political activities in opposition to the regime carried out by Italian migrants abroad deeply concerned the Fascist authorities. Il Duce not only personally resented the attacks on his regime by Italian anti-Fascists abroad, but was worried that such anti-Fascism could create the impression of a divided nation in which Fascism faced strong opposition. Italian consuls were instructed to fight anti-Fascism on all levels, for example by asking foreign governments to

*Members of the unofficial Fascist branch formed in Melbourne in 1925. Eustacchio Del Pin is fourth from the right. (*Italo-Australian*, 1925)*

expel 'those Italian agitators who are most active and who work for the perversion of the working masses'. Yet Mussolini's doctrines would soon be actively taken up by the majority of Italians in Australia who had migrated before the First World War, without having experienced in person the brutality and violence of the Fascist squads. Even some of those migrants who had been compelled to emigrate by the events of 1919–22 paradoxically accepted Fascism because in the actions and the rhetoric of the new Italian government they seemed to detect a new determination to defend their economic interests and political rights and to counter the threats posed to their religion, language and traditions by a largely hostile social and political environment. Fascism appealed quite successfully to the unsophisticated, scarcely educated migrants who were linguistically and socially insecure and isolated, targets of discrimination and abuse. Italians abroad in general, and in Australia in particular, fell for the Fascist rhetoric, the ceremonies, speeches and trappings of the regime, and its aggressive and bombastic style.

As early as 1923, an attempt was made in Adelaide to form a branch of the Fascist Party, and a branch was unofficially opened in Melbourne in October 1925 by a small group of sympathisers, led by Eustacchio Del Pin. The first official Fascist Branch was opened in Melbourne in November 1926 by the Italian Consul-General, Antonio Grossardi, in the presence of 400 Italians. Grossardi was a curious figure, typical of many diplomats, politicians and businessmen, who tried to ride the wave of Fascism in an attempt to control it—or perhaps more cynically, who always tried, desperately and obstinately, to side with whatever party was in power. Before 1922 Grossardi had been, like Mussolini, a Socialist; after 1945 he turned Christian Democrat, thus continuing his apparently inexorable long march towards a comfortable and well-rewarded career in the diplomatic service.

Consul-General Antonio Grossardi. (Italian Bulletin of Australia)

Italian Fascists at the ceremony marking the formation of the first Fascist branch in Australia. Melbourne, 1926. (Italian Bulletin of Australia)

Between 1926 and 1928 Fascist branches sprang up in Australia wherever there was a sizable Italian community. Their main supporters were wealthy Italians: greengrocers, traders, businessmen, importers of Italian foodstuffs, wool merchants, doctors, journalists, intellectuals and people who, for professional reasons, were generally in close contact with Italy and her diplomatic representatives in Australia. Their allegiance to Fascism was, at best, sentimental and irrational or, at worst, utilitarian, and was mainly expressed by wearing the black shirt and by raising their arms in the Fascist salute at the frequent rallies, celebrations, *feste*, marches and religious meetings, as well as at Anzac Day marches.

Their ideological confusion between nationalism and patriotism, Fascism and pragmatism nevertheless ideally suited the pursuit of their personal interests but was often disconcerting to the more orthodox, fanatically 'pure' Fascists like Sydney Vice-Consul Mario Carosi, or like diehard journalist Franco Battistessa, who was expelled from the Sydney Fascist branch because he was too much of an extremist even for the local Fascists' taste. Sometimes even the dour faith in Fascism of these businessmen was shaken by reasons other than ideological objections or pecuniary interest. When the wife of one of the leading Italian businessmen of Sydney was seduced by the Italian Vice-Consul, Buoninsegni-Vitali, a newspaper owned by the injured party became the most vociferous advocate of a radical shake-up and of the need to 'fascistise' the local Italian diplomatic representatives.

Another pillar of support for Fascism in Australia was the Catholic Church. Italian Catholic priests not only took part in Fascist rallies and gave sermons in praise of Fascism, but also openly supported Mussolini and his representatives in Australia. The Apostolic Nuncio, Bartolomeo Cattaneo, was very friendly with Mario Carosi and other Fascist leaders, and so was Sydney's future Archbishop and Cardinal, Norman Gilroy. Brisbane's Archbishop James Duhig was perhaps the most vocal prelate in praise of Fascism. He had been received by Mussolini several times, and would not miss an opportunity to come out in support of the slogan that every Italian was Fascist and that, by implication, whoever was not a Fascist was a bad Italian, a renegade, a Communist. This was precisely the line adopted by Fascist propaganda.

Because of the pervasive influence of Fascism within the Italian community, the sizable minority of migrants in Australia who were not Fascist, indeed who strenuously and courageously opposed this ideology, were often forced to contest and to fight their workmates, their neighbours, even their friends and next of kin. Undoubtedly,

Consul-General Mario Carosi (first from right) and representatives of the Italian associations in Sydney, arms stretched out in the Fascist salute, place a wreath on the Cenotaph on Armistice Day, 1929. (Italian Bulletin of Australia)

their intellectual leader was Omero Schiassi, a reader in Italian at the University of Melbourne. Schiassi had been actively combating Fascism in Italy before fleeing to Australia in 1924. A lawyer for the Socialist Trade Union Movement and councillor of the Bologna City Council, he had been a friend of Socialist leaders, including Matteotti and Mussolini, before the latter's defection from that party in 1913. Schiassi was a charismatic figure. Always impeccably dressed, he was a strange mixture: almost courtly in his manners, he was aloof and conscious of his intellectual superiority, yet he was a convinced Socialist, following the reformist trend. There was a big gap between him and the uneducated, barely literate Italian workers and businessmen, but he had a very dramatic imagination which found expression in rhetorical speeches which were admired, though often not understood, by ordinary Italians. Paradoxically, his addresses were attended even by the Fascists, mesmerised by the beauty and passionate rhetoric of his perfect Italian.

Yet the most controversial and active figure among the anti-Fascists was the anarchist Francesco Giuseppe Carmagnola. Born in the Veneto region of a humble peasant family, in Italy Carmagnola had been involved in active resistance to the Fascist squads and was compelled to flee the country in 1922. In Australia he was soon noted by the authorities for his political activities. In fact both the Italian Secret Service in Australia, the dreaded OVRA, and the Commonwealth Police kept an uneasy eye on the movements and the actions of this anti-Fascist. In 1927 and 1929 he founded two newspapers, *Il Risveglio* and *La Riscossa*. This so enraged Consul-General Grossardi that he succeeded in having *Il Risveglio* closed by

The anti-Fascist newspaper La Riscossa, *edited by Francesco Carmagnola, on the occasion of the sixth anniversary of Giacomo Matteotti's murder.* (New York Public Library)

the Australian authorities on the grounds that it was 'most dangerous and likely to inflame the minds of the Italians and cause a lot of trouble as it is openly inciting class warfare, bolshevism, anarchy, violence and political murders'.

La Riscossa was by far the more important of the two papers. Three thousand copies were distributed in Australia as well as to subscribers in France, the United States and South America. The distribution of *La Riscossa* took place even in places controlled by the Fascist authorities. In 1931 Carmagnola was able to distribute the newspaper among passengers and sailors of the Italian ships berthing at Melbourne. The most successful anti-Fascist enterprise launched by Carmagnola was the founding in 1928 of a club in Melbourne, the Matteotti Club, named after the Socialist leader murdered by Fascist assassins in Rome in June 1924. The Matteotti

Melbourne, 1928. Italian anti-Fascists at the Exhibition Gardens after the May Day Parade. Standing at the far right is Francesco Carmagnola.
(Cresciani Collection)

Anarchist leader Francesco Giuseppe Carmagnola while serving in the Italian Army, c. 1921. (Cresciani Collection)

Club was a meeting point for people who opposed Mussolini, a place where one could read anti-Fascist literature received from all over the world. Its members and sympathisers numbered 800 and were actively involved in marches, rallies and in collecting money for the families of anti-Fascists who were jailed in Italy, among whom was Sandro Pertini, who in 1978 became President of the Italian Republic.

For their part, the supporters of the Matteotti Club wanted action, not just words: they sought confrontation with the Fascists, and to this purpose went around in clubs and public places, armed with guns and iron bars, provoking Fascists to fight. On 2 February 1929, when the first talking picture was screened at the Auditorium in Melbourne, showing an address by Mussolini to the American people, Carmagnola and a few dozen anti-Fascists disrupted the show. Similar disturbances were staged during the visit of Father Salza, an agent of Fascist propaganda. In Ingham, Queensland, in November 1928, anti-Fascists gathered outside the building where he was lecturing and threw stones on the tin roof, causing panic among the audience. When Salza lectured at the Australian Hall in Sydney, about thirty anti-Fascists attempted to disrupt the meeting, but were confronted by the Fascists and thrown out.

The most remarkable incident was what the anti-Fascists later called the Russell Street fight. On 27 October 1929, at the Temperance Hall in Russell Street, while approximately 150 Melbourne Fascists, all wearing their black shirts, were celebrating the seventh anniversary of the March on Rome, they were attacked by Carmagnola and his men, who rushed into the hall and took them by surprise. Before they could realise what was happening, several Fascists were injured. The news of the fight quickly reached Sydney. The impact on local Fascists was such that many did not attend the local celebration of the March on Rome, held on 29 October, for fear of a similar attack from Sydney anti-Fascists, and many present at the celebration refrained from wearing the black shirt.

The years from 1928 to 1932 were the best years for the anti-Fascist movement: it reached its fullest capacity of action and influence, and the Labor Government, led by Scullin, was more sympathetic to the cause of Italian anti-Fascism than the previous Bruce Government or the later Lyons Government. By the early 1930s, the fires of the Depression were raging out of control. In the canefields of north Queensland, which had attracted many Italians who were compelled to seek work far from their homes, there was a strong nucleus of anti-Fascist sympathisers, and Carmagnola joined them.

Carmagnola addressing the audience at the Matteotti Club, Melbourne, on the occasion of the sixth anniversary of the murder of Socialist leader Giacomo Matteotti by the Fascists. 1930. (Cresciani Collection)

In Ingham, Carmagnola went on publishing his newspaper, *La Riscossa*, and in 1931 was involved in a serious incident when he and two other friends assaulted the Italian Vice-Consul, Mario Melano. At his trial, held in Townsville, Carmagnola took advantage of the proceedings to launch, to the astonishment of a hostile Crown Prosecutor and judge, a scathing attack on Italian Fascism. He was acquitted by a sympathetic jury composed mainly of waterside workers. Perhaps one of his more significant actions was that of taking a leading role during the great cane-cutters' strikes of 1934 and 1935, which led to the burning of the cane to rid it of the rats which were causing an infectious and fatal disease known as Weil's disease.

The 1930s, which saw the decline of a strong and aggressive anti-Fascist movement witnessed, conversely, an increase in the fortunes of Fascism. Not only had the Italian regime benefited politically and gained in respectability by signing the 1929 Concordat with the Vatican, which normalised relations between State and Church, but even its most reckless military and colonial adventures were now attracting wide support among Italians at home and abroad, as well as among foreign sympathisers.

Fascist expansionism found its enthusiastic admirers also among Australians, most notably among the returned soldiers, the Establishment and the middle class. One of them was Prime Minister Lyons. Joseph Aloysius Lyons had defected from the Labor Party in 1931 to form the United Australia Party and was to become Prime Minister following Labor's defeat in the election of December that year. He would remain in power throughout the Depression until 1939, during which period he was openly supportive of Mussolini's regime.

In 1932, the famous Harbour Bridge opening incident took place when Captain Edward De Groot rode up and cut the ribbon with

Italian Fascists in Sydney rally around Consul-General Agostino Ferrante. (Cresciani Collection)

his sword before Labor Premier Jack Lang could perform the task. De Groot was a member of the New Guard, an organisation set up in 1931, modelled on Fascist principles and a front for the less visible Old Guard; the latter carried on quasi-military reactionary activities and contained within its membership many prominent figures. They claimed 100 000 members who were rabidly anti-Communist. New Guard leader Eric Campbell wrote in his book *The Rallying Point* that, 'had communism been introduced into New South Wales either by act of Parliament or otherwise we would have crushed it, if necessary by force'. Yet contacts between Italian Fascists in Australia and members of the New Guard remained sporadic. The Australian right-wing organisation was not considered by the Italians as a serious interlocutor within the Australian political context. On the other hand, the New Guard did not seek the collaboration of the Italian Fascists out of detachment from anything which was alien, especially if coming from migrants who were considered by many Guardsmen as a backward 'race'.

The Australian Catholic Church also supported and legitimised Mussolini's expansionism. In 1935 Italy invaded Ethiopia to conquer for herself an empire or, as Mussolini put it, 'a place in the sun', vis-à-vis the other European Colonial Powers. As Italian tanks and aeroplanes were flung against barefoot soldiers, the Australian Catholic Establishment and Archbishop James Duhig in particular praised the aggression as enthusiastically as the Italian migrants who supported Fascism. They fell for the propaganda ploy that Italy was a Great Power and that Rome was spreading Christian civilisation among the heathen. Similarly, in 1936, when Mussolini intervened alongside Hitler in the Spanish Civil War, migrants believed they could now walk proudly among foreigners because they were the sons of a nation which was as good as others in flexing her military muscles, in imposing her will, in moulding world history.

Italian Fascists give the Fascist salute at the Sydney Cenotaph on Anzac Day, 1938. (Italo-Australian)

Melbourne's Archbishop Daniel Mannix backed Mussolini and Spain was seen sympathetically as yet another instance of Fascism's political and military might, a deadly struggle between Christianity and Communism, between civilisation and barbarism, between Rome and Moscow.

The Italian regime whipped up international support for its policies by means of a shrewd propaganda campaign and by indulging in the proven method of gunboat diplomacy. Faraway Australia was visited by the cruiser *Libia* in 1922 and the destroyer *Armando Diaz* in 1934. Again, in 1938, Australia was visited by contingents from many countries to celebrate the 150th anniversary of the founding of the colony at Sydney Cove. The Italians sent the cruiser *Raimondo Montecuccoli*, which had arrived from Spain where she had been shelling Republican positions. Archbishop Gilroy said Mass on board the vessel, and Prime Minister Lyons expressed 'his highest esteem for Fascist Italy and the Fascist Regime and his deep admiration for the Duce'.

It was in Melbourne, during the visit of the *Montecuccoli* to that city in February 1938, where the last significant episode of Italian resistance against Fascism in Australia took place. Carmagnola and a group of anti-Fascists went aboard the ship to conceal anti-Fascist propaganda. One of them, an Italian who had been naturalised, was caught by the crew and assaulted. The political uproar that ensued from the mistreatment of a British subject climaxed in a monster demonstration against the sailors of the *Montecuccoli*, during which Carmagnola harangued a crowd of 12 000 people and burnt an effigy of Mussolini.

Yet by the end of the 1930s, the inexorable march towards a European conflict undertaken by the Axis powers could be seen even by the most unsophisticated, uninformed observer—even by Italian migrants in Australia. Those who previously supported Fascism publicly were now trying to make themselves accepted by the Australian community or to disguise themselves by applying for a Certificate of Naturalisation or even by changing their surname into a French or English-sounding one. The anti-Fascists also had to face a hostile public opinion: their internationalism, their class-consciousness, the advocacy of violence, alienated and isolated them from the majority of the population. They were believed to be what the Fascists and the Consuls said they were: Communists, trouble-makers, dangerous people, whereas in reality they were only poor immigrants who came here to escape persecution and to improve their conditions. Anti-Fascists were frequently warned, in their own interest, to abstain from provoking further public disorders and from bringing into Australia their political wrangles and national divisions. Missing completely all ideological implications and historical realities, Australians believed that the place for Italians to settle their quarrels was Rome, and not Sydney or Melbourne.

A leaflet printed in Paris and circulated in Australia in support of gaoled Italian anti-Fascists. Gino Lucetti was an Anarchist, and Umberto Terracini was a Communist. The Socialist Alessandro Pertini, on the right, was jailed by the Fascist Government from 1927 to 1943. He would become President of the Italian Republic from 1978 to 1985. (Cresciani Collection)

By 1940, the indiscriminate hostility against Italians among Australians made anti-Fascist activity impossible and also pointless. In July Francesco Carmagnola was arrested at the Sydney Domain while he was distributing leaflets and carrying around a large cardboard poster with the inscription 'All Italians Are Not Fascist', and with caricatures of Mussolini and photographs of several anti-Fascists.

On 10 June 1940, before an immense crowd, Italian dictator and Duce of Fascism Benito Mussolini professed his lust for world power by declaring, from the balcony of the Palazzo Venezia, war upon France and Great Britain. At the same time, unwittingly and tragically for them, he had also declared war on the Italian migrants in Australia, both Fascist and anti-Fascist. Soon they would be looked upon as enemy aliens in a land which had witnessed the birth of their children, the sacrifices of their labour, the steadfastness of their determination to 'make good' for themselves and for their families, their sometimes ill-placed expectations of being given a fair go. Instead, internment, economic hardships and social dislocation would be the only reality facing Italians in Australia, the unfortunate victims of a global power struggle whose implications they could hardly understand.

5

ITALIANS AND AUSTRALIANS AT WAR 1940–1947

On 10 June 1940, the world had already been at war for over nine months. By then, the German armies had overrun Poland, Denmark, Norway, Belgium and Holland with impressive speed and efficiency and on 10 May had begun their *blitzkrieg* against France.

By contrast, Mussolini's Italy had been standing by, undecided whether to enter the conflict or to maintain her neutrality. Finally, apprehension of being denied her share of war spoils, concern at being seen by her powerful Nazi ally as lukewarm towards her obligations under the Pact of Steel, and fear of missing her chance to live her 'day of a lion', got the upper hand over military unpreparedness. On 10 June Il Duce broke all reservations and declared war on France and Great Britain.

News of Italy's declaration of war reached Australia at dawn of 11 June 1940, and the Italian consuls representing the Fascist Government in this country hurriedly burned their papers and documents minutes before the consulates were closed down by officers of the Security Service and Army Intelligence. The same day, in a secret cablegram to the Secretary of State for Dominion Affairs, the Australian Prime Minister, Robert Gordon Menzies, instructed the

British Government to indicate to the Italian Government that Australia, in association with Great Britain, was also at war with Italy.

Italy's entry into the conflict, though not unexpected, still caught some people by surprise. Until then, Italy was considered to be a faraway, second-rate country of no direct relevance to Australia. And as far as Italian migrants in Australia were concerned, they were seen just as another alien labour force which had to be assimilated into the mainstream of Australian society. However, by the beginning of 1940, the Federal Government became preoccupied with the matter of security. The possibility of sabotage, espionage, disruption to communications, the spreading of panic and false rumours was taken into serious consideration by the army which at this stage, together with Canberra, favoured limited and selective internment of those Italians who, whether naturalised or not, were considered to represent a security risk. Besides the obvious logistic and economic reasons against the uprooting and transporting wholesale of the entire Italian population to militarily secure concentration areas, an indiscriminate and massive internment of all male Italians was not favoured simply because not all of them were thought to be a threat to national security. This was not only the policy which the Federal Government wanted to adopt and would adopt, but was also the line followed by other Allied countries, in particular by Great Britain, whom Australia repeatedly asked for information in order to draft her own internment regulations, since it was considered desirable to have a uniform legislation throughout the Empire. In a letter to the Premier of New South Wales on this matter, Prime Minister Menzies unequivocally stated that 'since the outbreak of the war, the United States Government has approached the belligerents with a suggestion that mass internment should not be adopted. Germany and the United Kingdom have agreed to this, as has also the Commonwealth Government'.

The first Italians to become prisoners of war in Australia following the declaration of belligerency were the sailors of Italian ships berthed in Australian ports or sailing in territorial waters. The MV *Remo* was captured in Fremantle after its departure had been delayed for days by the Australian authorities on various pretexts. The MV *Romolo* had sailed from Brisbane on 5 June. On 12 June, however, she was located in mid-Pacific by the Royal Australian Navy vessel *Manoora*, whereupon the *Romolo* was set on fire by her crew and scuttled. The officers, crew and passengers, including two Italian migrants being deported to Italy, were picked up and brought to Townsville. Eventually they were transferred to the prisoner-of-war camp at Hay, New South Wales. Italian seamen of the cargo boats *Felce*, the Panamanian *Atlas* and the Norwegian *Anglo-Maersk* were also captured and interned on the first day of the war. The total

The scuttling of the Italian passenger ship Romolo *upon being intercepted in mid-Pacific by HMAS* Manoora. (Australian War Memorial)

number of Italian merchant seamen interned as POWs was 268. Eight women were not interned, and during the war four of them married British subjects.

For their part, Italian migrants in Australia, who had been forewarned by Fascist propaganda and by consular officials of the possibility of Italy's entering the conflict, were not surprised when they were visited, on the morning of 11 June, by police and Security Services officers who came to arrest them. Australian writer John S. Manifold, in a delightful short story entitled 'Fraser on Discipline', gives a festive and comical account on how the internment of Italians took place, with the unavoidable songs, salami and sly grog, and the detainees' explanations that their misadventure 'was anybody's fault except Mussolini's or Mr. Menzies' or world capitalism's'.

The reality was much duller. People were visited by plainclothes policemen, who also confiscated all papers, books, photographs and personal documents that they could find in the house, and were taken by car, taxi, bus or tram to local police stations, and ultimately to Long Bay and Pentridge jails where they were given the same treatment and food as the other inmates, locked up for more common and certifiable crimes. In the meantime, the wives, frightened that letters or newspapers overlooked by the searching police officers could be used, if found, to incriminate their husbands, took pains to destroy everything that was written in Italian. By 10 August 1940, throughout Australia, 1901 Italians had been arrested and put in internment camps.

Initially, conditions at Long Bay and Pentridge jails were very poor. Italian civilians under arrest were kept locked up in their cells from 4 p.m. until 7 a.m. each day and sometimes were compelled to sleep on a thin straw mattress laid on the cement floor. This treatment, as a worried NSW Premier's Department official admitted, was clearly in contravention of the provisions of the Geneva

Sydney, 11 June 1940. Police close an Italian fruit shop. (Sydney Morning Herald)

Convention. Food was equally poor. A German internee complained to the authorities that 'we were given ordinary prison food, which was often hardly eatable'. In some instances the prisoners were kept for two or three weeks before being transferred to the internment camps at Liverpool, Orange and Hay in New South Wales, Loveday in South Australia, Gaythorne in Queensland, and Tatura and Murchison in Victoria.

Sometimes Italians were interned not only because they were considered a security risk, but also as a measure to protect them from public violence. In June 1940, following some instances of intimidation against Italian shopkeepers at Bondi, in Sydney, forcing them to close their premises in fear of violence, and after the publication of two articles in the *Bondi Daily* and the *Balmain Observer*, which incited their readers to take direct action against the 'dagoes', the police were compelled to arrange for the publication of an article in the *Sun* on 20 June, warning people against taking the law into their own hands. In New South Wales, the situation was so explosive that Deputy Premier Michael Bruxner expressed his deep concern to the Premier, Alex Mair, that 'the feeling against disloyalists in this State has become so intense that disorder is likely to break out at any time, unless the fears of the community can be allayed by prompt action'. Yet with the exception of a few isolated instances, opposition to Italians was manifested mainly by means of repressed, contained hostility and resentment, rather than by overt acts of violence. Notwithstanding this, Military Intelligence, the Federal Government and many other bodies were worried that anti-alien feeling would turn into uncontrolled violence. Their concern for the safety of enemy aliens was motivated by the harrowing experience of World War I when instances of violence and harassment against German and Austro-Hungarian nationals had been so frequent that they had to be interned for their own protection.

View of the prisoner-of-war camp complex at Cowra, New South Wales. (Australian War Memorial)

Nevertheless, one wonders how genuine this concern was in 1940, since there is no evidence in State or police archives of any specific plan for the protection of enemy aliens, outside the standard police practices of supervision of crime prevention.

Most people, including State Government authorities, did not differentiate between Italian nationals and Italians who had been naturalised. It is indeed depressing to see government papers, with the significant exception of Security documents, rife with commonplace, irrational and sensationalist beliefs about Italian migrants, comprising a further indication of the lack of insight into the social, religious, political and community traditions of this large group of non-English-speaking migrants.

Although not everybody vented their prejudice in the simple, arresting words of that 'Australian mother' who warned NSW Premier Alex Mair to beware Italians, because 'once a dago or a German, always one', it was invariably, although covertly, there. Between 1940 and 1942 the Press and public opinion became increasingly jittery about the danger of Italians being potential saboteurs, terrorists and Fifth Columnists. There were countless instances of people reporting on Italian migrants' purportedly suspicious behaviour. Perhaps the most emblematic instance of collective paranoia against Italians at this time was that of an inhabitant of Nhill, Victoria, who wrote to the Prime Minister protesting against the fact that Italian enemy aliens were employed at Nhill, while Australian workers were unemployed. Department of Labour inquiries established that the people in question were only three, not Italians but Albanians, who were carrying out work at the local sewerage plant that no Australian wanted to take. The employment of Albanians, commented the investigator significantly, was 'necessary to ensure the safety of other workmen, as the work is dangerous'.

Who were the Italians rounded up on 11 June and in the following months? With the exception of a small group of intellectuals, Fascist officials, businessmen and journalists, the majority were unskilled people. A police report on the occupational characteristics of interned and non-interned enemy aliens shows that the main occupations were labourers, market gardeners, farmers, greengrocers, shop assistants and shopkeepers. Few police officers who had been in personal contact with the internees were convinced of their being an actual threat. For instance, a member of the State Advisory Committee entrusted to review the objections to internment commented that

> a large number of the objectors are fruiterers and others are in a very humble station in life. Almost all of them have a wife dependent upon them and several have young children. The evidence almost invariably establishes that the objector is industrious and law abiding; and apart from the faculty of making success of their business few have exhibited much mental acumen.

The same officer concluded that the internees were not a menace in any real sense.

The most distinguished Italian to be interned was Prince Alfonso Del Drago, of an old Roman family, who had been president of the Italian Ex-Servicemen's Association and a member of the Sydney Fascist Branch. Prince Del Drago had the honour of being the only internee whom the Italian Government attempted to exchange with Australian prisoners in its custody, but since Italy did not hold as prisoner or internee an Australian considered of sufficient importance, no exchange took place.

After the Japanese attack on Pearl Harbor, on 7 December 1941, the number of Italian migrants interned in Australia reached a wartime maximum of 4727, out of 14 904 Italian aliens registered by the Commonwealth authorities. Thereafter, as the danger of a Japanese invasion disappeared, they were steadily released, and by September 1944 only 135 hard-core Fascists remained in the internment camps. Paradoxically, not only Italians who were suspected of being Fascist sympathisers were interned, but anti-Fascist and Jewish Italians as well.

The doubtful logic behind this policy was that, according to the Director of Military Operations and Intelligence, the onus was on the Italian migrant 'to show that he is not likely to be influenced by the possible consequences to his relatives in enemy territory and that he has thrown his lot with this country to such an extent that there is no prospect of his yielding to pressure by the enemy'. In most cases this was quite an impossible task and, as a consequence, many innocent people who had been harassed by the Fascists were forced to share in the internment camps the same accommodation as their persecutors. One of them, Francesco Fantin, was even murdered, on 16 November 1942, at the internment camp of Loveday in South Australia.

Undoubtedly, internment was a trauma both for Italians who were interned and for those who were allowed to retain their freedom, to pursue a life which could by no means be called normal. The latter were utterly confused by the climate of hostility which surrounded them and tried to keep a low profile, retreating into the family circle and visiting only their closest friends. (Even this modest social activity was interpreted by some Australian neighbours as an example of their subversive, conspiratorial tendencies.) In Griffith, they avoided going to the township on weekends and on busy days, to prevent unpleasant incidents. It could be reasonably assumed that the bitterness caused by internment in June 1940 would favour the emergence of nationalist or crypto-Fascist currents among Italians, yet although a small minority most probably shared these feelings, fear, insecurity and apathy prevented any public manifestation of patriotism, even in an unorganised, emotional way. It is understandable, then, that to people interested essentially in work and the family, with no links at all in most cases with Italian officials in Australia or with Italy, the whole question of their being a security risk was absurd and incomprehensible.

Understandably, panic, prejudice, ignorance and racism magnified the threat that Italians were purported to represent to the security of the country. For the second time in twenty years, they experienced the uncomfortable feeling of being forced to wear a false cloak. They were dubbed terrorists, Fifth Columnists, dangerous elements, just as previously they had been falsely portrayed by the Fascist authorities as ardent supporters of the regime. Yet again, they were victims of the difference between reality and appearance. During searches carried out by police and security officers, not one cachet of arms or explosives was found in their possession, not one single plan of subversive or terrorist activities was uncovered.

Instead, as the World War unfolded towards the inexorable defeat of the Axis Powers, Italian migrants in Australia progressively came to be known for what they really were—poor, simple people who had been forced by intolerance, ignorance and need to migrate from their Fatherland to an alien country in search of peace, economic security and a future. In 1940 the hope of achieving these modest aspirations had been dashed, and life in the camps or in freedom amid an understandably hostile environment was the only reality that confronted them and would continue to confront them in the following five years.

Italian prisoners of war harvesting tomatoes at Yanco, New South Wales, under military supervision. (Australian War Memorial)

The second and by far the largest group of Italians held in captivity in Australia were the prisoners of war captured mainly in the theatres of operation of North and East Africa and sent to Australian POW camps. Early in 1941, the worsening military situation in North Africa compelled the British Command to evacuate all Italian POWs to safer areas in the Dominions. On 2 April 1941, Australia agreed to accept the custody of up to 50 000 POWs from the Middle East, and the immediate transfer of 2000 Italian POWs from Egypt. On 28 May 1941, they arrived in Sydney on the *Queen Mary* and were despatched immediately to the camp complex at Hay, which had been established in August 1940 at British Government expense. In June 1941, at Cowra, the largest complex of POW camps in New South Wales, with a capacity of 4000 people, began operating. By December 1941, a total of 4396 Italian soldiers and 561 officers had been transferred from Egypt to Australia, the bulk being detained in the two New South Wales camps. Other main concentration camps for Italian POWs were later established at Murchison, Tatura and Myrtleford in Victoria, at Loveday in South Australia and at Marrinup and Northam in Western Australia. Because of the shortage of ships, no other Italian POWs arrived in Australia by sea before October 1943. The POWs were being held by the Australian Government as agent for the United Kingdom Government, and all expenditure incurred and earnings credited were on the latter's account. The British agreed to pay for the maintenance of the prisoners a per capita rate of seven shillings a day.

The interests of the Italian POWs in Australia were safeguarded by George W. Morel, a Swiss citizen, delegate for the International Red Cross, who had his appointment officially approved by the Australian Government on 4 February 1941. For the duration of the war, Morel frequently visited all POW camps in Australia, compiling detailed reports for the International Red Cross Committee which contain invaluable information about the health of the prisoners, their accommodation facilities, instances of insubordination, food, work, sporting, spiritual and educational conditions.

In stark contrast to those for enemy aliens, conditions in the POW camps were good. Prisoners were allowed to read daily papers and periodicals after they had been censored, and could also listen to the radio. Accommodation and clothing were satisfactory and clean, food was excellent and abundant, with spaghetti and meat being invariably served every day—the menu had been fixed by common agreement between the authorities and the prisoners of war—and was cooked by Italian POW cooks. The POWs could also play soccer and tennis, grow vegetables within the camp compound and be involved in educational and artistic activities. Each camp had a well-stocked canteen, offering for sale foodstuffs, sweets, soft drinks, tobacco and articles necessary for everyday use. The health conditions, as reported by Morel, were 'on the whole' good.

According to Morel, there were a few unsatisfactory aspects of camp life which could have been easily remedied by the Australian authorities. The POWs wanted to send photographs to their families in Italy, and this could be done by arranging to have army photographers visiting the camps (this request was eventually approved by the army and official group photographs were taken and are presently stored at the Australian War Memorial). The mail service with Italy was most unsatisfactory, letters taking six months by sea or two by

Vegetable garden and a model of Rome's Coliseum built by Italian prisoners of war at the camp in Hay, New South Wales. Despite good imprisonment conditions, to many POWs Australia meant almost seven of the best years of their life spent in captivity, far away from their homeland, their towns and villages, their families and friends. Homesickness, as evidenced by this photo, was ever present, even when gardening. (Australian War Memorial)

air to reach their destination. In addition, the camps had almost no books to read with the exception of a few grammar and Latin books, received from Sydney University.

Italian POWs had been brought to Australia at the persistent request of the Federal Government, which badly needed manpower for its rural industry and war effort projects. In fact, on 2 June 1943, the Commonwealth Government approved the scheme whereby selected Italian POWs could be placed on rural properties in the custody of private employers, without guards, to relieve the manpower shortage and to increase production of vital supplies. Up to three prisoners were assigned to each farm, and were administratively controlled by a network of Army Control Centres. The Centres were also responsible for the POWs' welfare, for the recapture of escapees and for their disciplinary control. Compulsory drafting applied to soldiers only, while officers and NCOs were selected only if they volunteered. For their labour, the army paid one shilling and threepence a day for a six-day working week, and employers paid the Directorate of Prisoners of War £1 a week for each prisoner and provided for food and lodging. Prisoners could not be allotted to employers who were of Italian origin nor sent to areas with a substantial settlement of Italian migrants, and emphatically excluded from this scheme were 'active Fascists, agitators, bad workers or otherwise troublesome types'. Also, Italian POWs were not allowed to fraternise with civilians, 'particularly women'. The army took particular care to avoid confrontation on the issue of POW labour with the Australian Trade Union Movement, which objected to unfair competition from what was by many considered to be a modern version of slave labour—not without reason, since the cost of POW labour was much lower than that of civilian labour. By March, 1945, out of a total number of 18 432 Italian prisoners detained in Australia, almost 15 000 were working on the land, employed in rural work of great importance to Australian food production, without military supervision.

Undoubtedly, this scheme was a great success. Not only did the prisoners fill jobs for which Australian labour could not be found, and release from guard duties garrison troops who could be employed elsewhere, but also their economic contribution to the war effort was significant. For instance, Italian prisoners at Hay, New South Wales, were employed on a vast scheme of agricultural cultivation of over 1250 acres. In a few months, the entire countryside was transformed by the construction of a canal system of irrigation of a total length of about 90 kilometres. Tobacco, rubber and vegetables were being cultivated, and a model farm with 120 cows and 2000 chickens had been established. POWs were also employed in cutting down wood for the camps, maintaining a section of the Trans-Australian railway, roadmaking, brickmaking, soapmaking, carpentry, installing the sewerage system for the camps, and in projects aimed at making the camps as self-supporting as possible and to produce a surplus for army requirements elsewhere.

To many Italian POWs Australia meant that almost seven of the best years of their lives were spent in captivity, far away from their homeland, their towns and villages, their families and friends. Although, in comparative terms, the material conditions of captivity in Australia were vastly better than those endured by Allied prisoners at Coltano, Italy, Colditz, Changi or Dachau, the psychological, mental and physical stress of long years of confinement, isolation and meaningless life left an enduring mark on their characters.

Security Service reports and correspondence written by the prisoners of war give a somewhat sullen and at times tragic picture of Italian POWs' experience in Australia. Boredom, inactivity, lack of privacy and the frustration of camp life affected all prisoners sooner or later. In the microcosm of Loveday, or Myrtleford, or Cowra, the petty incidents and the events which occasionally took place were irrationally blown out of proportion. Depression, neurasthenia, exasperation and apathy were the most common forms of illness which affected the prisoners and which are mentioned recurrently in their letters.

For instance, a young Italian lieutenant wrote to his mother that, upon his return to the camp from work outside, he had 'the feeling of having arrived in an asylum of non-violent lunatics'. He went on, 'In our camp, there is a continuous, relentless struggle of the nervous system against the fence. The stronger ones win'. A more philosophical and articulate prisoner described to his brother-in-law, also a POW, in India, his daily life as follows: 'I read, play tennis, go swimming, curse my fate and Fascism in three languages and twelve dialects, grow pumpkins and flowers and await better times ... I get fat and stupid'. One of the best descriptions of the mental prostration which affected the imprisoned soldiers was written by a POW to his father in Rome.

> I believe that of all ... the prisoners like myself, three or more years of imprisonment on their shoulders, always shut in, few indeed can be considered as being perfectly normal in the head ... When, through necessity, I come into contact with my poor colleagues, I have the distinct sensation of being in a lunatic asylum ... When it is established with some friend that a colleague has gone out of his mind, we say with a certain coldness, that he has 'departed'. The day before yesterday we had the record because in the space of a few hours two of them 'departed', and thoroughly also.

Cases of insanity, both in the camps and on the farms, were not infrequent, though often not reported because of language difficulties or because the behaviour of the POW was considered strange, sulky, or even 'sly and objectionable'. Some of the most serious cases ended in suicide. Psychotic tendencies and neurasthenia sometimes ended in violence. In July 1944, at the POW camp at Hay, a prisoner was stabbed to death by a fellow POW, and another, again at Hay, was murdered in 1946. In July 1946 the camp commandant at Cowra requested the transfer from D3 compound (which hosted POWs with bad records such as escapees, insubordinate characters and would-be murderers) of three POWs who had threatened to kill the Italian camp leader. Mention is also made in despatches of instances of malingering, that is, of POWs who hoped, by self-infliction of injury, to be repatriated sooner than otherwise would have been the case. Five of these cases took place at Cowra in May 1943.

Italian POW eagerness to go out of the barbed wire on to the farms was invariably motivated by the desire to escape from the maddening life of the camps, to experience something different. This behavioural pattern explains also the infrequent yet significant instances of individual attempts to escape from the camps. By 1948, forty-one Italian POWs were still at large, nineteen of them in New South Wales, while attempts to escape from custody had taken place rather regularly in the preceding years. Life in a camp was so depressing that many, even proud and class-conscious bourgeois officers and Fascist diehards, volunteered to go on a farm, just to escape from the barbed wire. A number who accepted employment in rural industry were pleasantly surprised by the warmth and courtesy with which they were treated by their Australian hosts; others had mixed feelings, and a sizable minority was decidedly hostile. While some officers sincerely complained of the fact that 'whilst the Australian Command had promised us, among other things, quarters fit for civilized people, the majority of us found the lodgings indecent', objections to accommodation conditions or allegations of mistreatment (though in some instances correct) were usually the result of the uneasiness felt by Italian POWs in working for the enemy. Some of the POWs who had originally accepted employment on the farms justified their change of mind by putting forward incredibly imaginative stories. One POW, for instance, refused to work because he claimed his sleep was disturbed by the pet lambs walking about kicking tins, and the crowing of the roosters awakened him too early in the morning. Also, the endless years of imprisonment made many POWs desperately homesick and apathetic to whatever was happening to them.

Nevertheless, the majority of POWs enjoyed the opportunity of coming in close contact with Australian farmers. Some could not fail to notice the different customs and the different mentality. On the whole, most tried to make the best out of a difficult and depressingly protracted captivity. With typical Italian ingenuity, they were soon able to find loopholes in the system and to make themselves acceptable to garrison personnel and farmers alike. Intelligence officers and Control officers had a hard and, with hindsight, impossible task in trying to discourage fraternising between POWs, troops and civilians. At Leeton, POWs soon began trading in tobacco and cigarettes with the local population, at Cowra in rabbit skins. Also at Cowra, members of the AIF were purchasing beans from the POWs and selling them for a higher price to Edgells, while the POWs were receiving a cash payment much higher than their army pay. To the consternation of Intelligence officers, POWs at Cowra were not only smuggling correspondence out of the camp, eluding censorship, but also freely distilling *grappa*, the fiery northern Italian brew, for themselves and the garrison guards as well. At Wagga Wagga, Italian prisoners were served drinks at the local hotels after church, while at Coonabarabran they were seen in civilian clothes at the local picture show.

Edgardo Simoni, December 1940. One of the 18 432 Italian prisoners of war transported to Australia, Lieutenant Edgardo Simoni achieved notoriety for his many daring escapes from captivity in the camps and from the high security jail at Hay, New South Wales. He became a legend with the Australian military forces who, in awe and admiration for his Houdini-like skills, nicknamed him la volpe *(the fox). During his long periods of freedom, in Melbourne, Adelaide and Mildura, Simoni came in contact with many Italian migrants, who sheltered him, and with Australians, to whom he was cheekily selling insurance policies.* (Cresciani Collection)

Yet it was the problem of POWs fraternising with women that caused the biggest headaches to the military. At Orange, when the Control officer called in at the house of a resident, he found his daughter on the knees of an Italian prisoner in the lounge room, which was in darkness. At Tamworth, for a while, a *ménage à trois* did take place on a property, where a POW was sleeping with a farmer's wife, while the husband, fully aware of the facts, resigned himself to spending his nights in the car. The matter was hushed up by the military for the understandable reason that 'subsequent public ventilation of the facts may bring discredit on the farm scheme as a whole'. Indeed, reference to affairs between Italian prisoners and Australian women was made quite often in Intelligence reports, a fact that not only casts some light on the understandable frustrations of the POWs as well as the loneliness of some Australian women, but adds new meaning to the interpretation given by civilians to army instructions that Italians could not be driven, but could be led.

Whatever the benefits and despite some lighthearted aspects, a day in the life of an Italian POW in Australia was demoralising. Whether in the camps or on the farms, the impact of foreign customs and traditions, the inability to communicate in a foreign language, the limitations to their freedom, nostalgia for a normal, civilian life, preoccupation about their next of kin in Italy, caught between warring foreign armies in the south or tragic protagonists in the fratricidal civil war in the north, uncertainty for the future, were all factors that wore down the morale of the POWs, leading in the most serious cases to a progressive psychological erosion of their self-esteem, to neurasthenia and even to what was commonly called *morbus mentalis*, to insanity. Indeed, many soon found out that even going out to work on the farms, among strangers, was only a palliative, an alternative that was even harder to come to terms with, and preferred to be sent back to the confinement of the camps. The end of World War II meant to Italian POWs the conclusion of a tragic odyssey which had brought them to a land further away than any place they had ever dreamt of. Although many POWs expressed their wish to remain in Australia to work as civilians, their retention was not contemplated by Canberra, under the terms of the Geneva Convention. Repatriation began in August 1945 and it was not until February 1947 that all Italian POWs were returned to their homeland. Many of these returned soldiers would come back to Australia in the early 1950s as immigrants, often to go back to work on the same farms which had employed them as POWs during the War.

Ultimately, the presence of thousands of Italian prisoners had undoubted beneficial effects on Australian society and on the war economy. Their employment outside the camps, on projects of

Fifty-eight men and women at Parliament House, Sydney, after the lunch given in their honour by Premier Nick Greiner in June 1990. During the 1990s, the governments of New South Wales and Western Australia wanted to redress the injustice suffered by many Italian migrants and prisoners of war during the Second World War who had been interned for many years, even after the cessation of hostilities, without any evidence of their representing a threat to national security. Formal ceremonies and lunches were held at the Houses of Parliament for a representative group of ex-internees, and a monument to Italo-Australian friendship was unveiled in January 1997 at the former POW camp at Cowra, New South Wales. (Sydney Morning Herald)

national utility, not only defrayed the cost of their maintenance but contributed significantly to the supply of badly needed resources and services. Those on the farms relieved Australian labour and garrison troops for deployment to other areas or duties. Besides, the lengthy interaction between Italian prisoners and the Australian population succeeded to a large extent in dampening their mutual hostility, fed for too long by senseless Fascist propaganda on one side and xenophobic hysteria on the other. Ironically, the sudden injection of so many foreigners into the Australian social context, under the worst possible conditions, had the shocking but psychologically therapeutic effect of making Australians less jittery about the presence in Australia of a sizable non-English-speaking migrant component, and aware of the advantage, as well as of the necessity, of a large-scale immigration program after the war.

By all accounts, this was no mean accomplishment but a significant contribution to the material and spiritual development of Australia by the Italian prisoners of war, forced aliens in an alien land during the second world conflict.

6
MASS MIGRATION 1945–1971

When the war ended in 1945, Adolf Hitler's mad dream of world domination left humanity with a legacy of ruin and despair. For the second time during the twentieth century, Germany's quest for supremacy in the contest between the Great Powers had failed dismally, taking with it in its cataclysmic, Nibelungian end all its allies, like Mussolini's Italy, which out of fear, greed and ambition had sided with the brutal and implacable Nazi Siegfried. Throughout Europe, immense destruction was far outweighed by human suffering and social dislocation, the physical uprooting of millions of people, not to speak of the tragedy of the Holocaust.

Fascism's war caused widespread destruction to Italy's cities and her industrial infrastructure. The country suffered indiscriminate killing of civilians by Allied bombings, hunger and imprisonment, the ignominy of military defeat and the chaos of political, economic and social collapse. And it underwent the horrors of foreign invasion and civil war. With uncanny, paradoxical continuity, history seemed to repeat itself.

In September 1494, Italy had been invaded for the first time by the French armies of Charles VIII, with their Swiss mercenaries and formidable artillery, invoked by the Florentine Dominican monk and theocratic dictator, Girolamo Savonarola. Likewise, following the disintegration of the Italian State and Armed Forces, in September 1943 the peninsula was yet again invaded from the north by the Germans and by the Allies from the south.

For two years Italian soil became the battleground for the armies of at least a dozen countries as well as for Italians who fought against each other, siding with the foreigners on opposing ideological grounds. In the north, Mussolini invoked the assistance of his nefarious ally and advocate of a New Order, Adolf Hitler, to subjugate the Resistance movement and the Italian population, whom

Rome, September 1943. German parachutists search Italian civilians before deporting them to labour camps. (Oggi, 1983)

Il Duce by now considered spineless and unworthy of his despotic leadership. Yet, like Savonarola, who in May 1497 had been hanged and burned at the stake in Florence after the departure of the French armies, so Mussolini, abandoned by his German guardians, met his inexorable and violent end. In April 1945 he was captured by Italian partisans while trying to reach the Swiss border, wearing a German uniform, and was shot and hung by his feet, with his mistress and some of his diehard followers, in a piazza of Milan, where some months before fifteen partisans had been executed at German command.

His death heralded the end of Fascism, and the war, and the end also of an entire period of Italian history. Italians had been painfully immunised against the divisive and destructive disease of nationalism. By the end of 1945, 1.3 million Italian soldiers, who had been prisoners of war in many continents, began returning home. From the cruel snows of the Russian winter and the POW camps in Australia, India, South Africa and Canada, they returned to an Italy in ruins. One hundred and fifteen thousand were lost in Russia alone. Despite the propaganda, it was a war that most Italians never wanted.

Soon, to compound the human misery, the world would witness another scramble for power, another kind of war no less cruel: the Cold War, which would bring opposing ideologies face to face and would divide Europe into two blocs, the Soviet-controlled East, and Western Europe, allocated to the American sphere of influence by the Yalta Agreement. After 1947, as Winston Churchill dramatically announced in a historic speech at Fulton, Missouri, an imaginary yet tragically effective 'iron curtain' split the continent, from Stettin in the Baltic to Trieste in the Adriatic.

The millions of people who were displaced by these momentous and, to them, incomprehensible events, by this new alignment of

On 10 September 1944, during a raid on Trieste, two British bombers sank the liners Sabaudia *(30 000 tons),* Giulio Cesare *(21 000 tons) and* Caio Duilio *(22 000 tons). The photograph shows the burning Aquila oil refinery in the background, the harbour with the three capsized ships, and the Bristol Blenheim aircrafts flying over an old rice-husking factory, the Risiera, which had been converted by the Germans into an extermination camp. This was the only one in Italy, with a crematorium operating from 4 April 1944, in which more than five thousand hostages, partisans, political prisoners and Jews were incinerated.* (Cresciani Collection)

Great Powers, were forced to seek refuge in other countries. It was a desperate search for survival, security, freedom and lost families. Many of these unfortunate people were escaping from the gruesome reality of the Nazi-Fascist concentration camps, which had marked them forever, and from the irrepressible fear of ending up in Communist camps. Ironically, yet again they found shelter in communal camps, the refugee camps which mushroomed almost everywhere in Western Europe. Their dream was to flee as far as possible from war-ravaged Europe and from their nightmarish past to countries such as Canada, the United States and Australia.

At the same time, Australia's 7.5 million people were breathing a sigh of relief. Life was back to normal. The war had come perilously close. The threat of invasion, the bombing of Darwin and the penetration of Sydney Harbour by three Japanese midget submarines had taught Australians that their island was not an impregnable fortress, that the Royal Navy was no longer the invincible bulwark of Australia's forward defence line. Justifiable apprehension about national security unavoidably led many people to share an increasingly nervous realisation that their country was dangerously under-populated.

These strategic and geopolitical realities were highlighted even more by the fact that during the war economy period, Australia's industrial capacity and output had increased dramatically, and that

Milan under Nazi occupation. (*Oggi*, 1983)

after 1945 a hungry world was eager to buy more and more agricultural and rural produce. Suddenly people were struck by the incontrovertible evidence that the world had become much smaller, and realised the urgency and the need to increase significantly Australia's population, in order to bolster her defence capability and sustain her rapidly expanding industrial and agricultural economy. To this extent, the mutually convenient and converging needs of war-weary Europeans and Australia's population and defence requirements became official government policy. Incidentally, this policy served the always politically useful purpose of maintaining

The German Ambassador, Rudolf Rahn, with Mussolini. Between 1943 and 1945 Mussolini was the head of a puppet state in Northern Italy, the Italian Social Republic, which supported the Nazis in their struggle against the Allies and the Italian Partisans. (Oggi, 1983)

the myth of 'populate or perish', of exorcising the racist fear of a yellow peril threatening Australia from the north—fear which in this case was compounded by the fact that the 'Chinks' were also 'red'. In 1947, in an historical address, the Minister for Immigration, Arthur Augustus Calwell, announced that Australia was opening its doors to European migration, preferably British, but refugee and continental as well, although, as he said, 'It is my hope that for every foreign migrant there will be ten people from the United Kingdom'. Thus, between 1947 and 1971, Australia became involved in one of the most stimulating, challenging and irreversible experiments in social engineering in the world.

Australian immigration offices were opened throughout Europe to select, screen and recruit prospective migrants. People were given a most favourable, albeit utopian, account of Australia and of the economic possibilities open to them, and wooed to apply for a visa. During this period 2.4 million Britons and 800 000 non-English-speaking people emigrated to this country. Fares were heavily subsidised and assisted migrants paid £10 towards the cost of their journey. Certain groups, notably the British, were given preferential treatment.

After the war, Italy also began looking for overseas countries as possible outlets where Italians who could not find employment at home could go and settle permanently. In a controversial and irresponsible statement, Prime Minister Alcide De Gasperi in 1949 exhorted Italians to 'learn a foreign language and emigrate'. They did not need any spurring from their Prime Minister. Between 1947 and 1950, 20 000 Italians emigrated to Australia. In March 1951, Italy and Australia signed an Assisted Migration Agreement, whereby both countries, with the support of international agencies sponsored by the US Government, began financing the passage of Italian migrants. By 1973, from the end of the war, 305 000 assisted or

*Prince Junio Valerio Borghese (at the centre), Commander of the submarine
Sciré, which penetrated the Royal Navy bases at Gibraltar and Alexandria,
sinking the battleships* Queen Elizabeth *and* Valiant *and the cruiser* York. *After
Italy's surrender to the Allies in September 1943, Borghese joined Mussolini's
Italian Social Republic and its Nazi masters. At the head of a personal army
called Decima Mas, he fought against the Allies and Italian and Yugoslav
partisans. In May 1945 he was captured in Rome by the American Army. In
December 1970 he was the leader of the attempted neo-Fascist coup d'état
against the Italian Republic. After its failure, Borghese took refuge in Franco's
Spain. He died in Cadiz in August 1974.* (Oggi, 1983)

unassisted Italians, the largest non-English-speaking national group, had chosen this country as their new home.

At first, bureaucratic restrictions were imposed on people termed southern Europeans, which meant mainly southern Italians, who were only permitted to migrate if they had close family members already resident in Australia. This policy was undoubtedly a form of discrimination based on doubtful racial assumptions, a system of priority grouping which decided who should be admitted depending on whether they were considered 'European' or not. Indeed, as former Minister for Immigration Al Grassby pointed out,

> It was a completely racist policy in which base-grade clerks were making decisions as to who was substantially European. It was absurd and in that context, of course, the Italians suffered also because they were not in a priority group at all. They had to struggle and scramble to get equality. It wasn't until 1969, for example, it was recognized that Italian immigrants also had families. And it was not until then that they had the right, in fact, to assistance which had been given to everybody else in northern Europe and Britain, to bring their families with them.

As the rules for Italians were relaxed, the Government sponsored migrants, providing they stayed for a minimum two years. In return they were given a work contract and promised jobs.

Migrants in Trieste, 1954, board the MV Toscanelli, *bound for Australia.* (Cresciani Collection)

The cultural shock of arriving in a country vastly different in climate, customs, religion, language and even food made a lasting impact on Italian migrants. Many were unable to adjust to the change and returned to Italy as soon as they could afford the fare. The fact that the picture of an antipodean Camelot, spread by Immigration Department propaganda, was totally at variance with the reality faced by virtually all migrants is not surprising. Whereas great effort and money were spent in attracting people to Australia, virtually nothing was done to assist them once they arrived. There is no doubt that the Government was ill prepared for the influx of these people into Australian society; no structure with trained people had been set up to help them, and interpreting and translation services were virtually non-existent. People who sought work and accommodation, the things of immediate concern to them and their families, were unable to communicate with employment officers. Police, welfare agencies, trade unions, government offices, hospitals, schools—none catered for their needs.

Temporarily housed in former internment camps and army camps now hastily converted, often only by name, into migrant hostels at Greta, Liverpool, Villawood, Bonegilla, many Italians found it difficult to adapt to the new experience of communal living: to the stench of food cooked in dripping, to mutton, to the isolation from the Australian community, to the problem of finding a job, of creating for themselves, without help, a new life. Their problematic 'new beginning' in the 'land of the future' was masterfully portrayed in the picture *Silver City*, directed in 1984 by Polish-Australian Sophia Turkiewicz on a screenplay by eminent Irish-Australian writer Thomas Keneally.

At times, migrant alienation and frustration could not be contained any longer. At Bonegilla, perhaps the most notorious of these migrant concentrations, in July 1952 2000 Italians rioted against

A group of displaced persons from Europe soon after their arrival at an Australian migrant hostel. (Cresciani Collection)

camp conditions, lack of work and assistance to find it, and against the allegedly false pretences under which they had been induced to emigrate. The police intervened and the army was alerted. Two hundred armed troops and five tanks remained at the ready at the nearby Bandiana military camp.

An Italian eyewitness, Valentino Sartoral, evoked those days in chillingly vivid terms:

> To describe Bonegilla is hell: ten thousand of us complaining every day we want the job or repatriation. Two months of terror, there in Bonegilla, we used to live with five bob a week. It was winter: cold, humid, and we went through such depression, emotional depression. You were there alone, lonely. Nobody, it looked like, took care—everybody say tomorrow and tomorrow. There were a lot of young, just married men or something like that, which left wife, sister, mother in Italy. And,

I remember one in particular, who decided to end himself. And one morning there was a lot of confusion and they find this young man, hanged. And I think the cause was he was fairly depressed and he couldn't pay any debt that he left in Italy. We were very disappointed because Australia for us young, represented a dream. It was the Promised Land of Australia everybody talks about, you know. I hang on, I was only eighteen. But, God, it was a disappointment, this Promised Land!

Again, migrant riots took place in October 1952 in Sydney, where hundreds of unemployed Italians marched in protest on the city from the migrant hostels of Matraville and Villawood. These were by no means isolated incidents. In 1961, again at Bonegilla, migrant unrest once more ended in violence, and a few years later serious disturbances took place at the Ford car assembly plant.

Despite disappointments and setbacks, jobs were eventually found, lives reorganised. The trauma of hostel life was replaced by a different and bigger trauma as soon as the migrant left the hostel in search of work, lodging and an identity outside. Only half-baked attempts were made to prepare him for this experience, to give him the necessary key to understanding the society to which he had been persuaded to emigrate.

Like his predecessors before the Second World War, he soon found that the promises of quick fortune and happiness in a rich, easy-going, hospitable land were just vain promises. He realised that he was expected to cast away his personality, his language, his traditions in order to 'assimilate', that is to become similar to people whom he could not even understand, whose values and attitudes were as strange to him as his were to them. It did not take him long to understand that difference breeds diffidence and that he was

Aerial photo of Bathurst Army Camp, taken c. 1943 from an army aeroplane, before the camp was converted for use as a migrant reception and training centre. (Bathurst Tourist Bureau)

One of the early migrant hostels being set up after the Second World War. (Cresciani Collection)

not welcome, that he would always, at best, be considered a 'New' Australian, at worst a dago, a wog.

The fact was that the migrant had all the cards stacked against him. Church, trade unions, police and Public Service attitudes, State legislation on health, housing and schooling were invariably ignoring the needs of the migrant community, which were understandably greater than those of the Anglo-Celtic population. Italians could not understand the priest in church, the doctor at the surgery, the mate at the workplace. Often they were subjected to the degrading experience of having their children interpret for them.

Migrants were encouraged to learn English by officials of the Department of Immigration, yet the few language schools expected people with little more than elementary education, even in their own language, to attend classes after long hours spent on the factory floor. State Government agencies also ignored the problem, believing that the responsibility lay with the Federal Government which had allowed them to migrate in the first place. A sad and significant commentary to the whole situation is the fact that the first to recognise the migrants' need to communicate were the banks.

Non-government attempts aimed at smoothing the migrants' culture shock during the early stages of settlement also failed dismally. Although filled with good intentions, the activities of bodies like the Good Neighbour Council and the New Settlers' Association did not bridge the cultural gap, directed as they were almost exclusively towards Anglo-Celtic migrants. Italian migrants, as a matter of course, were not assisted to integrate, let alone participate, in the life of Australian society.

Nowhere was this sense of isolation and of frustration felt more intensely than in the schools and in the homes. Italian children were, at times, victims of vicious discrimination by teachers and pupils alike, just because they could not speak English and had different habits. Quite often they were assigned to a low-grade class because they were considered intellectually inferior or because it was too bothersome to cope with their particular needs. At home, in the absence of an infrastructure encouraging social interaction between Australians and migrants, the wives of Italian migrants were completely isolated from the environment in which they lived. They could just as easily have been on Mars.

Italian women, both old and young, were especially disadvantaged. If they were young, they were strictly shielded from contact with boys as traditionally they would have been in Italy. Marriages often continued to be arranged for them and suitable partners were brought from Italy. Older or married women, secluded in their homes, were alienated to an even greater extent. They were not even exposed to the limited social interaction their men experienced at work, in the factories and in the pubs. They bought from Italian stores and their contacts were confined to Italian-speaking shopkeepers and tradesmen. It was virtually impossible for them to learn English and this led to their being estranged from their own children who often refused to speak Italian in a blatant, pathetic attempt to cast away their 'Italianness' and to disguise themselves as Australian, to avoid being discriminated against.

The young, unmarried Italian male population often found themselves rejected by Australian girls. Normal interaction between the sexes being denied to them, groups of young men gathering outside cafés and on street corners resorted to making unwanted gestures at passing women. Australian girls who became involved with Italian men were discouraged, to say the least, from marriage. In Australian pubs, brawls were frequent between groups of Italians and Australians, young Italians often retaliating to abuse and slur.

The 'wogs' or 'wops' or 'dagoes' were despised and their humiliation found outlet in anger and violence.

The only thing that was plentiful and easy to get was work, especially of an unskilled or semi-skilled nature. Migrants were told to go out, get a job and make good for themselves, but when many did just this, they often attracted the wrath of Australians because they were working harder. The majority were engaged in large industrial development projects, which were rapidly absorbing increasing numbers of workers at a time when the Australian economy was rapidly expanding and diversifying from its hitherto agrarian nature.

Often the migrants were forced to travel in search of work, from the canefields of north Queensland to the vineyards and orchards of South Australia and New South Wales, from the railway building sites of Western Australia to the eastern seaboard cities, where employment could be found in factories, milkbars and local councils. Italians were among the migrants who built the Trans-Australian railway, the large power stations, dams, bridges, harbours, mines, powerlines and the Sydney Opera House.

The great project which reflected the spirit of the time was the Snowy Mountains Hydro Electric Scheme. Italians and migrants from many countries found employment on the 'Snowy' and worked under conditions and in jobs that most Australians preferred to avoid. Wages were high and after some years of hard work they saved enough money to establish their own businesses, to buy their own homes, or to return home. The Snowy symbolises a period from which, despite the odds stacked against them, most Italians would emerge as citizens of Australia. In spite of their being required forcibly to 'assimilate' against their wishes, they had often willingly integrated into a society that had hardly wanted them in the first place.

An Italian cane cutter in north Queensland in the 1950s. If it was the discovery of gold in Victoria in 1849 and in Western Australia in 1891 that brought many immigrants to Australia, it was undoubtedly the cutting of sugar cane in northern Queensland that attracted the bulk of them until 1956, when mechanised cane-cutting was introduced. Italian migrants were employed as cane-cutters as early as 1873 and 1882. From 1891, when the first batch of 335 contracted Piedmontese arrived in Townsville to join the 200 already there, the number of Italians in Queensland grew to about 2000 by 1925. This was certainly not a great number, but during that period they had managed to buy almost a third of the entire register of cane farms. Of about 150 plantations, fifty-two were Italian-owned. (Courtesy Alfredo Garipoli)

They overcame resentment, social isolation and cultural alienation to achieve a degree of economic security for themselves and their children equal to any in Australia. 'It's amazing how they survived this tragedy', commented Franca Arena, former member of the New South Wales Legislative Council and a Bonegilla migrant herself,

Italian cane-cutters in North Eton (Mackay), North Queensland, on 15 August, 1929. (Centro Studi Emigrazione, Rome)

how they were able to cope with all these difficulties, how they were able to settle down and—if I can use an Australian expression—work their guts out in this country, to make a better future for their children. I think that really what motivated people to survive in often so alien surroundings was this thinking of the future of their children. It was so important for them to succeed. And they accepted any sacrifice in order to succeed.

Among the main employers of Italian labour were the giant Broken Hill Proprietary Company, with its plants at Port Kembla, Newcastle and Whyalla, the car-manufacturing industry at Sydney, Melbourne and Adelaide, and the successful, emerging Italo-Australian companies which specialised in the construction of transmission lines, buildings and power stations, such as Transfield, Electric Power Transmission, Ascom, Grocon and Multicom.

Despite the failure of the assimilationist philosophy and despite the sense of personal, social isolation and cultural alienation experienced by the majority of Italian migrants, Australia essentially meant to them the possibility of achieving economic security and a dignity of life which had eluded them in their country of origin. Indeed, a few were remarkable success stories.

The brothers Bruno and Rino Grollo, sons of Luigi, who in 1928 emigrated penniless from Treviso to Melbourne, from a small concreting business created a civil engineering empire, Grocon Construction Pty Limited. During the last thirty years they built the largest buildings in Melbourne, among which are the Rialto building and the AU$2 billion Crown Casino, and in Sydney the Westin Hotel in the historic General Post Office building.

In Sydney, in 1956 Franco Belgiorno-Nettis and Carlo Salteri founded Transfield Pty Limited. During the 1950s, Australia's post-

An Italian labour camp at Menai, New South Wales, in 1951. The newly arrived migrants were employed in the construction of electric power lines. (Courtesy Camillo Di Rocco)

Italian labourers pouring concrete on a construction site in Sydney in the 1950s. (Courtesy Camillo Di Rocco)

war economy boomed and Transfield grew rapidly. New businesses were added, including bridge building, aircraft manufacture, galvanising, general construction and steel fabrication. In 1987 the company financed and built Sydney's second harbour crossing, the Harbour Tunnel, and in 1989 was awarded a AU$6 billion contract to build ten frigates for the Royal Australian Navy. In 1961 Franco Belgiorno-Nettis, who always distinguished himself as a patron of the arts, founded the Transfield Art Prize, and in 1973 established the largest Australian visual arts event, the Biennale of Sydney. In November 2002 the Australian Constructions Association bestowed on him the 2002 Services to Construction Award.

Sir James Gobbo, born in Melbourne in 1931 from Venetian parents, served as Governor of Victoria from 1997 to 2000. He was also President of the Italian Historical Society of Melbourne from 1980 to 1993. In 1998 he was awarded an honorary law degree from the University of Bologna. Currently he is chairman of the National Library of Australia, the Order of Malta, the Order of Australia and the Australian Multicultural Foundation, and he is Commissioner for Italy for the State of Victoria.

Sir Tristan Antico, who built from nothing the largest concreting business in Australia, Pioneer Concrete Services, and became renowned for his horse-breeding business, was the son of Anarchist Giovanni Terribile Antico, a migrant from Piovene in the Veneto region, who used to play the piano in the orchestra of the Anarchist Matteotti Club in Melbourne, with young Tristan sitting by his side.

Italians brought to Australia not only their skills and their labour, but also their politics, eating habits, values, customs and traditions. The 1950s and 1960s saw the mushrooming of Italian clubs, of Italian sporting associations, of religious festivals, of Italian newspapers, of the 'Little Italies' of Leichhardt and Coburg. In some respects they tried to re-create in this country a lifestyle which reminded them of their Italian village life before their departure. In doing so, they deceived themselves and their Australian friends in believing in an illusory, obsolete image of Italy, a country which in the meantime had also evolved and changed significantly. Today, therefore, most behavioural, moral, social, political and even linguistic patterns shared by many Italians in Australia reflect an Italy which has long disappeared, an Italy which nowadays has adopted values similar to those of contemporary Australian society. No wonder that many Italian migrants come back to Australia after a trip to Italy remarking disappointedly that 'Italy has become like Australia'.

Historically speaking, Italian mass emigration to Australia ended in the early 1970s when the economic situation and standard of living in Italy improved dramatically as a result of the 'Italian economic miracle' of industrialisation. Ironically, it ended just when

A group of Italian workers and their families relax at a picnic in Sydney, in January 1956. Italian families kept their traditions alive in their own homes, clubs and cafés. Imported Italian food and wine were readily available at local stores. The postwar period also saw the steady increase of locally produced Italian commodities. By the 1970s, the most superficial aspects of Italian culture, such as food and folklore, were integrated into Australian life.
(Cresciani Collection)

multiculturalism was announced as a policy under the Whitlam government. In an historic turnaround, Australia finally and officially recognised what she had in effect always been, a multinational community representing the cultural tradition of almost the entire world. The 'high priest' and spokesman for migrant causes was the irrepressible and flamboyant Al Grassby, who took every opportunity to fight for ethnic rights. During 1972–75 Grassby served as Minister for Immigration in the Whitlam Government. Today, the Italians in Australia are an old community, out of touch with the present Italian reality, a community which is divided, apathetic and uninterested in expressions of Italian life such as politics, culture and current affairs—with the exception of food and soccer. Attempts aimed at awakening and stimulating the migrants' interest in the political and cultural reality of Italy so far have had limited success. Their apathy and alienation for their country of election has extended also to their country of origin.

The end of mass migration in the 1970s coincided with the emergence of the manufacture of ethnic myths aimed at validating the Italian contribution to Australia's development. Al Grassby was one of the earliest and most vocal proponents of this new course, when in 1978 he declared that 'it is essential for Italian migrants to elaborate mythologies that will legitimate and give prestige to their historical presence in Australia'. No doubt he was inspired by the teachings of distinguished French semiologist Roland Barthes, who in his 1957 seminal book *Mythologies*, stated that 'myths are a way of communicating a message, a means to say something significant, a form as an instantaneous reserve of history, as available capital'.

Almost by definition, myths are inaccurate or simply untrue. One of the myths promoted in the very recent past is that of the inflated numerical strength of the Italian community in Australia, in the misconceived belief that numbers mean power. The Hon. Franco Danieli, Italian Under-Secretary for Foreign Affairs, in October 2000 boasted of Italian people's power in Australia, of 'a component of "Italianness" ... of over one and a half million ... approximately ten per cent of the entire Australian population'.

In reality, data from the 2001 Census indicate that migrants born in Italy totalled only 218 718, and that people living in Australia who declared having an Italian heritage totalled 800 256. Data for the third generation were not collected. Most of the second generation reached the age of procreation in 1996, while the first generation had outlived the childbearing stage.

The hope in a future that will witness a sizable third generation is therefore ill founded. The fertility rate of Italo-Australian women (1.55) is lower than the Australian national average (1.75), though higher than the Italian one (1.18)—the lowest in the world after Spain. The 1996 Census also forecast that 20 per cent of women of Italian background would not bear children. Therefore the myth that the Italian demographic presence is larger than it actually is, and that it will become even larger by reason of a third-generation baby boom, with a consequent increase in cultural, economic and political power and influence, is not supported by the available statistical data.

Another myth which needs debunking is the one that maintains that Italians in Australia have done well, have achieved a high standard of living and have secured a better future for their children, who in the main are successfully working in the professions. Reality is more complex than this stereotype would lead us to believe. Again, the data of the 1996 Census are indicative. The majority of Italians (62.6 per cent) have a weekly income lower than AU$300, while the national average is 50.8 per cent and that of people born overseas, other than Italians, is 52.8 per cent. The lower income of Italians is also due to the fact that 31.3 per cent have reached the age of 65 and their lower level of education has placed them in poorly paid jobs and made them more exposed to retrenchments. Also, 4.5 per cent of men and 7.3 per cent of women have never been to school and 49.3 per cent of men and 53.2 per cent of women left school before the age of 15. Although they migrated to Australia long ago, 20.6 per cent do not speak English well and an additional 2.9 per cent do not speak it at all. Older women have the lowest English proficiency; 42.4 per cent of Italy-born women aged 65 years and over cannot speak English well and a further 12.1 per cent cannot speak it at all. These low levels of English proficiency reflect low educational standards and possible inadequacies in the provision of English training when Italian-born women arrived in Australia in the 1950s and 1960s. Italian migrants were also the product of a society where illiteracy was and still is rampart. The 1991 Italian Census recorded the appalling figures of 1.2 million illiterate Italians, while another 6 million have not completed primary schooling and a further 17 million have only completed such schooling. At home, 83.7 per cent of first-generation migrants speak Italian (or, one suspects, what they think *is* Italian, that is their ancestral dialect), while only 40.2 per cent of the second generation speak it.

Second-generation Italians do not tend to marry people of another ethnic background. In 1991, 50 per cent of women and 47 per cent of men married other second-generation Italians. In the same year, only 5.8 per cent of people born in Italy married people born in Australia, the latter mostly of Italian descent, which indicates that almost the entire second generation has both parents born in Italy, but that approximately only one third of the third generation will have both parents of Italian background. This trend will unavoidably contribute to compromise the maintenance of Italian cultural traditions in Australia.

This overall picture not only invalidates any unrealistic expectation of a community in exponential, irreversible ascendancy in terms of people, power and persuasion. It also betrays a complex reality where there are success stories, great opportunities, social mobility, political stability, trust in the future, but where there is also sacrifice, failure, delusion, suffering, alienation, discrimination, isolation, poverty and nostalgia. Whoever interprets Italian exuberance, expressed during religious *feste*, rallies or celebratory functions, as a manifestation of achievement, of fulfilment, of commitment and participation in the affairs of the society in which they live, fails to understand the complex nature of the Italian character, which rightly believes that reality is not just what one sees on the stage of everyday life, but, much more, is the perennial struggle within ourselves between the incontrovertible greed of personal interest and the somewhat deceitful projection of our existential, whimsical, propitiatory public image. The colourful outbursts of patriotism and religiosity during the visit to Australia by Italian President Giuseppe Saragat in 1967, by Pope Paul VI in 1970, by President Francesco Cossiga and Premier Giulio Andreotti in 1988 and by President Oscar Luigi Scalfaro in 1998 must be viewed in this context. In any event, active involvement by migrants in Italian politics was always discouraged and opposed by the Australian authorities. During the 1950s and the 1960s, the Australian Embassy in Rome screened prospective migrants, and membership or even association with members of the Italian Communist Party, as well as suspected collusion with the Mafia, were *prima facie* reasons for being refused an entry visa to Australia.

Sometimes threats were also made to deport uncomfortably active left-wing Italians, and in 1978 the Fraser Government actually deported an Italian journalist, Ignazio Salemi, for political activities carried out as a leader of the pro-Communist Italian Federation of Migrant Workers and their Families. The right-wing Italian Press in Australia, controlled by the local Italian Establishment, lobbied persistently in favour of such expulsion. Signor Salemi was not new to experiences of this kind. He had already been expelled from a Communist country, Czechoslovakia, when, in 1968, while in Prague as a correspondent for the Italian Communist paper *Unità*, he threw a flower pot on the head of a policeman arresting one of the supporters of Alexandr Dubček, the deposed prophet of Communism with a human face.

Efforts to spread Italian culture among Italian migrants in Australia has received lukewarm support among the latter. Activities promoted and financed by private enterprise, such as Transfield's Art Prize and the Sydney Biennale, are primarily staged for the benefit of cultured Australians. Yet finally it is in the field of cultural exchanges that Italy, Italians in Australia and the Australian community can look for positive and lasting results. The bringing together of the two cultures, the improvement in the perception of each other's intricate and complex realities, a better understanding of Italy's and Australia's needs, expectations and hopes are tasks whose achievement can ultimately have a deep, beneficial effect on the economic and political relations between the two countries.

The instruments to achieve these tasks, the policies to realise a closer cultural interchange have been in place for a long time. On 28 May 1975, Prime Ministers Gough Whitlam and Aldo Moro signed in Rome an Agreement of Cultural Co-operation between Australia and Italy, 'recognising the contribution of the Italian migrant community to the diversity of life in Australia [and] inspired by a common desire to promote and develop closer social and cultural relations in the future'. The Agreement has been regularly renewed. On 6 February 1997, Foreign Affairs Ministers Alexander Downer and Lamberto Dini signed in Rome the already mentioned joint declaration on Australia and Italy into the 21st Century, to 'ensure that our bilateral relationship remains dynamic and meets its full potential'.

Under the umbrella of these international agreements, during the 1980s and 1990s cultural exchanges flourished, promoted by the two Italian Institutes of Culture in Melbourne and Sydney and by a host of other organisations, among which several stand out: the Italian Historical Society; the Victoria University, with its Italian Australian Records Project, established with funding from the Australian Research Council; the Italian Australian Institute in Melbourne, whose founding chairman is Rino Grollo; and in Sydney the Italian Committee of Assistance, the Italian Historical Society and the Italians in the NSW Project of the State Library of New

South Wales. Besides, in 1999 the Cassamarca Foundation of Treviso established eleven lectureships in Italian at Australian universities, supported for the first triennium by a grant of AU$3 million.

Particular mention must be made of the Frederick May Foundation for Italian Studies of the University of Sydney, founded in 1976 and dissolved in the year 2000, which aimed to make Italian culture known in Australia by direct links with Italian institutions and scholars, without the dominant Anglo-Celtic mediation, as previously had been the case. During its existence, the Foundation organised four major international conferences, in 1978, 1980, 1982 and 1986, published a dozen books on multidisciplinary issues and invited to Australia the best names of Italian culture, among whom are the historians Renzo De Felice, Giorgio Spini, Giuliano Procacci, Emilio Gentile, Franco Venturi and Vittore Branca; the philosopher Remo Bodei; the economists Paolo Sylos Labini and Nobel Prize winner Franco Modigliani; the linguist Tullio De Mauro; the semiologist Umberto Eco; the literary scholars Alberto Asor Rosa and Claudio Gorlier; and the sociologist Francesco Alberoni.

During the same period, major cultural events were staged by Italy in Australia. In 1988, on the occasion of the bicentennial celebrations of the birth of European Australia, the Italian government organised 'Italy on Stage. Italy Salutes Australia's Bicentenary', a multimedia event that included a concert at Sydney Opera House by the Orchestra of Santa Cecilia, a recital by soprano Katia Ricciarelli, exhibitions, theatre, music and a film festival. A similar robust presence was made on the occasion of Sydney's 2000 Olympic Games, with tenor Andrea Boccelli as the leading star.

Art exhibitions proved the most popular and successful medium. In 1982 Sydney University hosted *Spelt from Sybil's Leaves. Explorations in Italian Art*, an exhibition from the Padiglione d'Arte Contemporanea in Milan. The Art Gallery of New South Wales has staged several exhibitions with Italian themes: in 1988 *The Renaissance in Venice*, in 1995 *Renaissance Drawings from the Uffizi*, in 1997 the painter Giorgio Morandi, and in 2002 *The Italians*, a major review of three centuries of Italian art. In September 1994 the Australian Museum in Sydney hosted *Rediscovering Pompeii*, a large collection of Roman objects and art; in 1997 the National Gallery of Victoria displayed *San Marco and Venice*, and in 2000 the Powerhouse Museum of Sydney exhibited *Leonardo Da Vinci. The Codex Leicester*. In 2002 the Museum of Contemporary Art of Sydney put up an exhibition on *Arte Povera. Art from Italy 1967–2002*, from the Castello di Rivoli Museo d'Arte Contemporanea in Turin.

During the last twenty years, stimulating cultural impact has also been given by the visits and lectures of prominent Italian architects

Capuchin friars build a church in North Queensland, c. 1950. Italian clergy from different orders had been ministering to Italians in Australia since the 1840s. Italian and Spanish Benedictines arrived in Western Australia in 1849 and founded the New Norcia monastery, while Elzeario Torregiani was the first Capuchin bishop in Australia from 1879 to 1904. Several Capuchin friars arrived from the United States in October 1945. During the 1930s, migrants were assisted spiritually by Jesuit father Ugo Modotti, while the Scalabrinian order sent missionaries to this country in November 1952. (Cresciani Collection)

such as Paolo Portoghesi; Renzo Piano, who designed the Aurora Place skyscraper in Sydney; Mario Bellini, who designed the AU$136 million extension to the National Gallery of Victoria; and Gae Aulenti, who in November 1993 spoke to 400 people at the Museum of Contemporary Art in Sydney. Also of iconic importance was the appointment of Maestro Gianluigi Gelmetti as Chief Conductor and Artistic Director of the Sydney Symphony Orchestra in 2004, and the selection of Italo-Australian artist Patricia Piccinini, born in Reggio Emilia, to represent Australia at the Venice Biennale in June–November 2003.

However, despite this significant Italian cultural and artistic presence in Australia, despite the receptive environment of 800 256 people of Italian ancestry living in Australia (4.21 per cent of the population), as evidenced by the 2001 Census, despite the over 700 Italian sporting, recreational, social, cultural and religious associations established all over Australia, despite the hundreds of Italian business concerns affiliated to the network of Italian Chambers of Commerce in Australia, it would be difficult to maintain that Italian influence has made significant inroads into the prevailing Anglo-American public culture of Australia. Food, feet and folklore are still widely considered as being the sole contribution made by the Italian migrant to the common good. One of the top-rating popular songs in Australia in November 2002, by the evocative title 'It is Un-Australian', is singing the praises of chauvinist values that one hoped had been forever relegated to a forgettable past, a past that saw for too long colourful anti-Italian stereotypes, vicious products of parochialism and prejudice, dominating some aspects of Australian life unchallenged. Far too often, whenever there was political or economic capital to be made, the stereotypes were produced by intolerant and insensitive men. In his novel *They're a Weird Mob*, published in the 1950s at the peak of Italian migration to Australia, author John O'Grady spelled out what most Australians expected at the time from those recalcitrant and unconforming newcomers:

> There are far too many New Australians in this country who are still mentally living in their homelands, who mix with people of their own nationality, and try to retain their own languages and customs. Who even try to persuade Australians to adopt their customs and manners. Cut it out. There is no better way of life in the world than that of the Australian. I firmly believe this. The grumbling, growling, cursing, profane, laughing, beer drinking, abusive, loyal-to-his-mates Australian is one of the few free men left on this earth. He fears no one, crawls to no one, bludges on no one, and acknowledges no master. Learn his way. Learn his language. Get yourself accepted as one of him; and you will enter a world that you never dreamed existed. And once you have entered it, you will never leave it.

Fortunately, most Italians were proof against this *cri de coeur*. They preferred to keep their ancestral traditions although they were manifestly receptive to the best that Australian culture could offer—though not the jingoistic mateship of the 1950s, or the prosaic, populist nationalism of the 1970s, or even the Hoganist ockerism of the 1980s and the racist ramblings of Pauline Hanson and her One Nation Party in the 1990s! With their work and sacrifices they earned the right to recreate for themselves an identity, a dignity, a way of living within a foreign society which persistently demanded their 'assimilation' but was not, until recently, far-sighted and challenging enough to afford them unconditional life membership.

In many respects, this challenge is today more relevant than ever to Italian migrants. Only by being fully aware of the fact that their Italian heritage enhances Australian culture, only by not feeling

Italian migrants at a naturalisation ceremony in Sydney in the 1970s. The grafting of Italians into Australian society was not without problems. Many immigrants refused, and still do, to accept and to identify with values and customs with which they feel uncomfortable. The serious act of renouncing their nationality, and the adoption of the Australian one, was the symbolic turning point that many immigrants were not prepared to take. As at 1997, one in three Italian-born migrants still did not take up the Certificate of Naturalisation. (Cresciani Collection)

inferior but by exercising their political, economic and social rights and duties, can Italians in Australia acquire that sense of Australian identity, or social equality, which will enable them to take part, freely, on equal terms, in all aspects of Australian life. Otherwise, they will always feel relegated to little ghettos, little Italies, little multicultural enclaves, which serve only the purpose of concealing an unpalatable reality and of defending entrenched interests.

Until Italians, be they in Italy or Australia, become aware that they must exercise their political power, in future things will change only to remain the same, as prophesised by Tomasi di Lampedusa in his novel *The Leopard*.

7
FULL CIRCLE

Today Australia is a pluralist, multicultural nation. More than fifty years of sustained immigration of people from more than 140 different countries has radically changed its character. The world has become smaller and has moved closer to these shores. Whatever happens elsewhere has immediate repercussions in Australia. The great social, political and economic issues besetting the world have become Australian issues.

Conversely, the Italians, who for just over 120 years have literally been *cives orbis*, citizens of the world, forced as they were to scatter abroad in a migratory diaspora of unequalled proportions, today are no longer venturing their lives in alien lands. On the contrary, they witness the phenomenon of return migration and enjoy a degree of unprecedented economic security, as the fifth or sixth industrial power in the world, as a respected member of the G8, the exclusive club of economic giants. For those who resisted the temptation to emigrate, Italy is today, if not the most comfortable in economic terms, undoubtedly one of the most dignified, humane and civilised places to live in.

A civil society, indeed, yet one which is not easy to understand. Italian affairs, economics, social, industrial and interpersonal relations remain today in the mind of the foreigner almost as impossibly puzzling as they must have been to the eyes of the countless invaders, conquerors, allies and 'liberators' who have descended on the peninsula since the time of the Renaissance. Italian politics in particular are extraordinarily abstruse and are invariably permeated by a veneer of unfathomable, Byzantine complexity, which defies understanding even by seasoned Italian political analysts.

A country where the average lifespan of a government between July 1946 and May 2001 was barely twelve months, Italy would give to the superficial observer the impression of being politically unstable. In effect, with the exception of the former Communist Bloc countries, Italy has been politically, until the 1990s, the most stable country in Western Europe. Nowhere else has the same political party been firmly in power, either alone or in a coalition, from

Italian terrorists shoot at the police in Milan during violent extreme left-wing demonstrations in 1977, during which the policeman Antonio Custrà is killed. (L'Espresso)

July 1946 to April 1992, as has the Italian Christian Democratic Party. It is a fact that from 1946 to 1992, Italy has had forty-eight governments but only eighteen prime ministers, sixteen of them Christian Democrats. Some of them served as prime ministers several times: Alcide De Gasperi served seven times, and so did Giulio Andreotti; Amintore Fanfani served six times, Aldo Moro and Mariano Rumor five. Besides being prime ministers, these Christian Democrats also took charge of several ministerial portfolios in other governments led by their Party colleagues.

So stable, almost unmovable, was the Italian political system until 1992 that its politicians had to resort to imaginative political formulas to explain away to the electorate the ingenious and, to them, profitable game of political musical chairs they were engaged in, and to simulate changes that did not take place. Thus the government formed by the Catholic Christian Democrats in alliance with the Marxist Socialist Party in the 1960s was called a government 'of the converging parallels', while that which saw the unofficial 'historical compromise' between Christian Democrats and Communists at the end of the 1970s was described as one 'of national emergency'. Yet another coalition was proclaimed as fostering 'more advanced equilibria'. Even in more recent times, the craft of formulating illogical or contradictory political theorems, in order to justify to the electorate betrayals or sudden changes in political alliances, was dear to Italian politicians. In 2002, Premier Silvio Berlusconi spoke of 'variable geometries' to pave the way for the scaling down of his controversial ally, the Northern League.

In effect, from the 1940s to the 1990s, nothing changed. Power was firmly in the hands of the Christian Democrats. Giulio Andreotti, a crafty Christian Democrat who led seven governments, began his political career in 1946 and was firmly in power in the 1950s, when Churchill was British Prime Minister, Nehru was ruling India and

Demonstrators and police clash in 1960 during the riots that occurred when the Government of Christian Democrat Ferdinando Tambroni was voted into power with the support of the neo-Fascist Movimento Sociale Italiano. (L'Espresso)

Soekarno Indonesia, when Eisenhower was US President, Adenauer West German Chancellor and Khrushchev just beginning his struggle for supremacy in the Kremlin. In 1992, when all these leaders had long disappeared from the political scene, Andreotti was still running his seventh prime ministership. His is the witty yet quite apt remark that 'power wears out only those who do not have it'. Other facetious Christian Democrats fully endorsed the dictum coined by Italian *politologo* Giorgio Galli, who in 1966 characterised Italy as an imperfect democracy, where the party in power is condemned to rule forever and the ones in opposition are resigned never to achieve power.

Political stability, albeit concealed under layers of shady party deals, compromises, appearances covering different and differing realities, was also reflected by social stability. Alarmist headlines in the international Press during these years persistently yet erroneously conveyed a doomsday impression of the Italian situation. Indicative of this effect are *Time* magazine cover stories on 'Italy in Agony' (18 November 1974); 'Italy: the Red Threat' (14 June 1976); 'Italy vs. Terror' (22 May 1978); 'Why Italy Works. Land of Miracles' (17 August 1981). *Newsweek* magazine also rivalled its American competitor in sensationalism with its cover story of 1 August 1977 entitled 'Italy: Living with Anarchy'. In some way, the mesmerising character of Italian affairs was still eluding the editors of the international press twenty-five years later. One had just to read *The Economist* survey of Italy (7 July 2001) under the heading 'What a lovely odd place!'

Despite vocal concerns expressed by the international Press and, more significantly, by a number of Western governments, the Italian State was able to crush political terrorism, from both the Left and the Right, to avoid its disruptive effect on the social fabric of the nation and to overcome this terrible period of its recent history by defeating and relegating Fascist terrorism and the Red Brigades to the dustbins of reactionary and proletarian revolutionary history. This was possible to a large extent because of the crucial support given the Government by Italy's powerful Communist Party—yet another paradox—which declared officially its support for the NATO Alliance and for the continuation of the American presence in Europe against the Red Army.

The collapse of Communism, symbolised by the fall of the Berlin Wall on 9 November 1989 and by the formal demise of the Soviet Union on 8 December 1991, had a profound influence on the Italian political system. The Cold War motivations for social revolution, such as anti-Communism and the threat of invasion, which bound together the ruling coalition parties in a conspiracy of interest, ceased to exist. A signal emblematic of the crumbling of the old world was Premier Andreotti's dissolution, in November 1990, of the Gladio-Stay Behind clandestine organisation, a secret corps of 622 volunteers who would have carried out sabotage and resistance activities in the event of Soviet occupation of Italy. After more than forty years of stifling 'First Republic' party dealings, the genie of change, of honest politics was let out of the political Pandora's Box. Italians no longer had to endure the stench of corruption for reasons of *force majeure*; no longer were they forced, as encouraged by conservative journalist Indro Montanelli, to vote Christian Democrat 'while holding their nose'.

In 1992, investigating magistrates in Milan, the most popular and effective being Antonio Di Pietro, began uncovering a series of bribery scandals. The city soon became known as *Tangentopoli* (Bribesville) and under the operation *Mani Pulite* (Clean Hands) many leading politicians, public servants and businessmen were arrested and imprisoned. By mid-1993 more than 200 members of Parliament were under investigation, including seven former ministers, among them former prime ministers Bettino Craxi (Socialist Party) and Giulio Andreotti (Christian Democrat). The magistracy made also calamitous mistakes and continued to imprison people before trial and release them only when they denounced others. They came to be seen by some as politically tinged, draconian inquisitors, part of a plot to ensure a judicial path to power.

The political parties were dissolved in disgrace, some to reappear under new and fanciful names like Ulivo (Olive Tree), Margherita (Daisy), Democratic Party of the Left, Alleanza Nazionale (National Alliance), Partito Popolare Italiano (Italian People's Party). New political parties emerged, like Forza Italia (Go Italy), later to be reconstituted as La Casa delle Libertà (Freedom Alliance), financed and led by business magnate Silvio Berlusconi, and the Lega Nord (Northern League), led by Umberto Bossi, who accused the national government of squandering northern wealth on the south, advocated a new constitution with a federal Italy divided into three autonomous republics, and rabidly opposed foreign immigration. Bossi's main electoral plank was 'devolution', that is the granting to regional governments the powers—until then jealously maintained by the national government—to manage education, health and the police. Many politicians feared that 'devolution' in effect meant 'dissolution' for the Italian State. Under the 'Second Republic', which ostensibly started in 1992, most politicians of the ancien régime recycled themselves into the new system in a classical exercise of *trasformismo* (transformism).

The new face of Italian politics was undoubtedly Silvio Berlusconi, Italy's richest man, a media mogul who built from nothing Fininvest, a vast financial empire employing 30 000 people, and portrayed himself and his party as an efficient and businesslike alternative to the corruption and cronyism endemic in Italian politics. Italians voted for him in the mistaken assumption that an enormously wealthy man had no need to steal from the public purse, and also because Berlusconi blatantly promised to make them millionaires (he promised to raise the monthly basic retirement age pension to one million old lire). At the elections of 28 March 1994, he led Forza Italia to victory and became Italy's fifty-first prime minister in an unholy alliance with the neo-Fascist National Alliance and the separatist Northern League. However, the new Prime Minister's honeymoon was short-lived. In December 1994 magistrates formally questioned him on alleged business malpractices. Faced with a no-confidence vote and with the unexpected defection of Bossi's unpredictable Northern League, the great populist communicator resigned on 22 December 1994.

In June 2001, after five years of Left-wing administrations, Berlusconi formed his second government, again in coalition with his former untrustworthy allies. However, the taint of the indictments of conflicts of interest, money laundering, tax evasion, business malpractices, illegal political donations and complicity in murder and bribery of politicians, judges and the finance ministry's police did not go away. On 28 April 2001 the *Economist* published a survey under the judgmental title *Fit to Run Italy?*, questioning his ethical credentials and his pledge to carry out a thorough revision of the judicial system because of its alleged political bias. These concerns were well founded. Two of the Bills approved by Parliament in 2002 were in fact aimed at extricating Berlusconi from his legal quagmire. One was the decriminalisation of fudging or falsifying company's ledgers, the other, the Legge Cirami (Cirami's Law), allowed defendants to repeatedly seek the transfer of their trial to other, more sympathetic courts which, because of the lapse of time since the offence, could apply the statute of limitations. Under the Italian penal code, this extinguishes the crime.

The arrogance of power of the new masters, their unashamed manipulation of the media, the demonising of the judiciary, the use of the state as a tool to pursue personal interests, were strongly condemned by Claudio Magris in an article in Milan's daily *Corriere della Sera* on 20 November 2002, in which the eminent intellectual spoke of 'a new frontier of intolerance, where the borders of decency are being dangerously shifted. Responsible for this involution is a new class—crass, indifferent to any civic, democratic value, to the principle of political commitment as an asset and to any idea'.

The leader of the Neapolitan Camorra, Raffaele Cutolo, and his associates are being brought to trial. Both Mafia and Camorra organisations operate a sophisticated network of activities ranging from prostitution to protection, from drug and weapons trafficking to the control of sections of the building and banking industries. (Courtesy Giovanna Borgese, *Un paese in tribunale*, Mondadori, 1983)

The morass in which the executive, the legislative and the judiciary were precipitated was perhaps symbolised by the Andreotti affair. Giulio Andreotti, a perennial symbol of Italian politics and widely rumoured of having been the *éminence grise* behind every deal, scandal, plot and machination for more than forty years, in 1996 was put on trial in Palermo, accused of criminal association with the Mafia. The prosecution claimed that in 1979 he had ordered the murder of a journalist, Mino Pecorelli, who was going to expose

Andreotti for protecting and abetting the Mafia's criminal activities and expansion, in exchange for its 'arranging' political support in Sicily. It was also alleged that when, in 1992, Andreotti broke this pact, the Mafia showed its 'displeasure' by killing the Mayor of Palermo, Salvatore Lima, Andreotti's Christian-Democrat Sicilian pro-consul. At the trial which ended in 1999, Andreotti was acquitted *per insufficienza di prove* (because there was insufficient evidence), but a subsequent trial in Perugia, in November 2002, following the confession of Mafia *pentiti* (turncoats), the 83-year-old life Senator was sentenced to a 24-year jail term.

The trials, even if not demonstrating conclusively Andreotti's guilt, did expose the cancerous collusion between Mafia and the political and administrative institutions of the state. It evidenced the enormous and pervasive power of this criminal *piovra* (giant octopus), as Italians are wont to call it, which used hearses and coffins to traffic in arms and drugs throughout Italy. In 1993 Mafia-planted car bombs did great damage to the world-famous Uffizi Gallery in Florence. But it is the spectacular murders that are the hallmark of Mafia activity. In 1979 they did away with Boris Giuliano, chief of Palermo's Flying Squad. In 1982 they killed Carlo Alberto Dalla Chiesa, the Piedmontese General of the Carabinieri, who had previously crushed Red Brigades terrorism and captured their leader, Renato Curcio (Dalla Chiesa had been posted to Palermo to fight the Mafia). And in 1992 Italy's top investigators of the Mafia, Judges Giovanni Falcone and Paolo Borsellino, met their death at the hands of the Mafia.

Another racket from which criminal organisations are drawing their power and influence is the illegal construction of housing. Between 1996 and 2001, according to Legambiente, an environmental protection organisation, 191 667 homes, apartments and villas were built illegally, for a total of 26 million square metres, the equivalent of 3183 soccer stadiums. The threat to their owners of having them demolished is negligible, 0.97 per cent. In Sicily, Campania, Calabria and Apulia, which host 37 per cent of illegal constructions, facing the criminal protection practices of Mafia, Camorra and 'Ndragheta, local authorities are powerless to impose the rule of law.

In contrast with the inertness and crystallisation of the political system, Italian postwar reconstruction and rapid economic development exposed the country to enormous changes which dramatically and permanently altered its social structure and way of living. The ravages of the Second World War left Italian industry, then as now situated mainly in northern Italy, largely destroyed. The government decision to reindustrialise rapidly not only the areas of the north but also selected areas in the south was taken in 1948, after Prime Minister Alcide De Gasperi returned from a trip to the United States, where he had been promised massive economic aid through the European Recovery Plan then being launched by Secretary of State George Marshall. The recovery was assisted also by the rigid wage structure to which the Italian workforce would be constrained for the ensuing twenty years, which assured Italian industry cheap labour and competitiveness on the world export market.

The 1950s and 1960s saw the Italian economy expand at an impressive rate equal only to that of Western Germany and Japan. Gross domestic product grew by an overall 5.9 per cent per annum during this time, reaching a peak of 8.3 per cent in 1961. This was mainly due to the efficiency of Italy's new plants; to the centralised nature of the economic system, in which the state owned or had a controlling interest over 50 per cent of Italian business, thus facilitating economic planning; and to the popularity of Italian-designed products and to the containment of wages and salaries. Many economic commentators spoke at the time of an 'Italian economic miracle', which exposed the country, with sudden and pervasive efficacy, to consumerism and technological change. In social terms, Italy, and the south in particular, jumped from a traditional agrarian stage to the age of the computer without going through the long stabilising and settling stage of an industrial revolution which in other European countries had produced a large, skilled, urban middle class and had drastically changed the old class structure and class values. Today, especially in the south, the old reassuring way of life often coexists with the dynamic new in glaring contrast. Nowhere is this more visible than in the southern city of Matera, where life in the *sassi*, the primitive dwellings carved out from the side of the mountain, goes hand in hand with the life of consumerism, of boutiques, jewellery and high fashion, in apparently inexplicable contradiction.

In the drive towards industrialisation, it was the underdeveloped south of Italy which attracted much attention and a great deal of resources. Change had always been alien to the southern ethos and had always come—often been imposed—from outside, from the north and from Rome. Bossi's often proffered complaint against *Roma padrona* (bossy Rome) is attracting considerable grassroots support. Nevertheless, some of the postwar changes, though unobtrusive, were by no means less important. For instance, the introduction and use of the insecticide DDT in 1945 by the Allied Armies defeated malaria in the south, a plague which had marred those regions for centuries, while the beginning of national television broadcasts in 1953 contributed more to unifying the south and the rest of the country than the efforts made and the energies spent in this direction by the many Italian governments of the previous hundred years.

In 1950, the Italian Government, in order to secure rapid and widespread industrialisation of the south, set up the Cassa del

Mezzogiorno (Southern Development Fund). Between 1950 and 1984 the Cassa spent 94 000 billion lire (approximately US$78 000 million) in a commendable effort to create an industrial backbone for these regions. Huge industrial complexes were built in Taranto, Naples and Gela, though, it must be said, often without due consideration for local environment, social or even market conditions. Italians aptly called them 'cathedrals in the desert'. Money was lavished on the construction of public works, roads, hospitals, bridges (25 per cent); on industrial (23 per cent) and agricultural (21 per cent) development; on the tourist, fishing and craft industry (15 per cent); and on job training (paradoxically, a mere 1.88 per cent).

To a large extent, the aims of the Cassa del Mezzogiorno were not achieved; the south was not transformed into a new industrial haven but remained what it had always been: a society ruled by a macroscopic, non-productive network of assistance to the private sector, either state-organised or Church-sponsored, Mafia-imposed or privately promoted. In its thirty-four years of operation, the Cassa was able to create only 780 000 new jobs—too little too late to stem the haemorrhage of southern labour to the factories of the industrial triangle of Turin, Genoa and Milan and to catch up with the developed north.

Besides, in the absence of a capital-producing economy, assistance has always come hand in hand with political patronage and often criminality. Even today, jobs are frequently given to people who support the local political boss and it is a well-known fact that it is extremely difficult to find employment without a *raccomandazione*, a reference. This explains why even some highly automated industries like the Fiat car plant at Cassino, near Naples, have an inexplicably large labour force. Traditionally, the Italian state is perhaps the most lavish promoter of such a welfare mentality, unable as it is to create fast enough new jobs for people entering the labour market. It is widely known, as evidenced by 1997 official government statistics, that 20 million Italian workers generate wealth to pay for 21.5 million pensions for people who often benefit from them without any legitimate rights. Sadly, it is also a well-known fact that in cities like Naples and Palermo, criminal organisations are the largest job creators and employers. Romantically and rather simplistically called Mafia, these gangs seek to control the protection and drug trades, and operate, to all practical purposes, as an efficient and smoothly run multinational business enterprise. It has been estimated that the drug traffic passing through southern Italy is in excess of US$10 billion annually. Sociologists reckon that over 10 per cent of the labour force in Palermo is directly or indirectly controlled by the Mafia. The gang warfare which ravaged Naples during the 1980s and which resulted in more than 1500 killings began when the local criminal organisation, the Camorra, stepped in to take control of the building industry and of the billions of dollars poured into the region by the Italian Government in aid of the 1982 earthquake victims.

Thus it became inevitable for the southern unemployed, even for the *assistiti*, to look north in order to improve their lot. The drain from the south to northern Italy as well as abroad was enhanced in 1956 by Italy's entry into the European Economic Community. The creation of a Europe-wide economic market further stimulated her economic recovery and also opened the doors of other countries to the Italian worker, who could now go there freely and find work at wages higher than at home. In fact the industrialisation push of the 1950s and 1960s had several marked and interconnected effects on Italian society: it created enormous shifts of population, from the south to the industrial areas of northern Italy, to the mines, factories and steel mills of Germany, France and Belgium and, incidentally, also to Australia. Between 1963 and 1973 more than 5 million people left the south of Italy in search of work elsewhere.

The second effect was to depopulate the Italian countryside. Peasants and farmers in the north as well as the south were attracted to the northern cities where they could earn much higher wages than by working their poor plots of land. The effect of this exodus was to concentrate 90 per cent of the Italian population on 25 per cent of the national territory. In 1997, only 6.8 per cent of the workforce was employed in agriculture. The foreseeable outcome of this inevitable trend was that, by the early 1970s, from a country exporting agricultural produce, Italy became an importing nation, whereby in 1997 she had a net deficit of 18 000 billion lire on imported food and agricultural produce.

It was in the northern factories that the ugliest consequences of industrialisation were most felt. Often southern workers were treated as mere 'factory fodder' and experienced the inhumanity of rapid, uncontrolled development, and isolation in an environment foreign and hostile to them, the alienation of cultural values different, if not altogether antithetic, to the ones cherished by their traditional rural culture. They became migrants and foreigners in their own country. Yet it was the labour of the southern migrant in the north which contributed significantly to make Italy the fifth or sixth industrial power of the world. It was his remittances to his loved ones still living in the southern villages and cities, together with the social security system, which to a large extent enabled the south to survive.

Notwithstanding the heavy price of emigration, alienation and exploitation, Italians in the north and south alike have improved their standard of living so dramatically that today few Italians still emigrate internally or go abroad in search of work. Indeed, the phenomenon of return migration that began in the 1970s is

The founder of Transfield, Franco Belgiorno-Nettis. Australian industrialisation in the 1950s and 1960s saw the formation of large Italo-Australian business concerns. Civil engineering companies like Ascom, Electric Power Transmission, Grollo Constructions, Tenix and Transfield monopolised the construction of shipping, buildings, power lines, power plants, communication infrastructure and services. Transfield, which began operating in 1956 with a jeep and £10 000, is today the largest privately owned Australian business. Its proprietors, the Belgiorno-Nettis family, have a turnover of AU$1.3 billion and employ over 8000 people. They are also important patrons of the arts, sponsoring the Biennale of Sydney and several other cultural initiatives. (Transfield Group of Industries)

nowadays an established pattern. In 1995 the National Institute of Statistics registered 43 303 Italians who permanently transferred their residence abroad, against 96 710 who returned to Italy. As Giorgio Napolitano, a former Communist leader, reluctantly admitted, they never had it as good as under forty years of corrupt Christian Democrat rule. For many Italians, the dream of becoming *signori*, of becoming middle class, had already turned into reality. Urbanisation, consumerism, the media and communications revolutions, the welfare state and widespread government assistance to industry all made it possible for most people to achieve a level of social security unequalled in the history of the country, to the point that in 2002 the public debt totalled 1386 billion euro, approximately 47 million old lire for every inhabitant. Since the late 1960s, Italian workers have enjoyed rights and privileges unparalleled in Europe. The Statute of the Workers practically bars employers from retrenching workers, and workers retrenched from companies in liquidation are supported by the state, through the Cassa Integrazione system, by receiving, for nine months, 80 per cent of their last salary. Social security and invalid pensions are so perversely and universally granted by the patronage system that millions of people receive them without legal entitlement. In 1996 it transpired that out of 7 million Italians drawing disability pensions, many were doing so illegally. In the Post Office, where the racket first came to light, ninety-four out of one hundred employees taken as 'invalids' were found to be healthy. Computer checks on a larger scale quickly brought an army of some 28 000 'invalids' into the sights of the judiciary. Many more were suspected of being in hiding. The main cogs in the fraud included bribed officials or doctors, some of whom participated by resuscitating the medical records of the dead.

Despite the economically and morally dubious practice of bestowing pensions on clients and protégés, thus expunging them from official unemployment statistics, the search for a job, for a *posto*, is still the crucial preoccupation in the life of the young Italian. In fact unemployment has steadily risen from 7.5 per cent in 1979 to 12.2 per cent in 1984, to remain at 12.2 per cent in 1996, when three-quarters of the 2.8 million unemployed were people under 30 years of age, concentrated mainly in the southern regions. The Press regularly reports extreme and absurd instances of job hunts, such as the one that took place in Rome in January 1981, when 32 000 people applied for the eighty-six vacancies in the urban police, or the one that occurred in Milan in April 1984, when 15 000 jobless contended for the one hundred positions as cleaners and labourers advertised by the City Council, or the 18 000 applicants for the twelve jobs as skilled workers at the Palermo Post Office in June 1984.

Yet official figures and sensationalist instances of collective job hunting can be deceptive to an uninformed observer. For years there has existed a 'submerged economy', whereby people out of work find easy employment in enterprises that do not ask workers to pay taxes, while employers do not pay them the official award rates, or social security, health or retirement benefits. This huge section of the Italian economy, the so-called *'lavoro nero'*, 'black' work or 'black economy', employs more than 8 million Italians, who contribute to the national estate for an estimated 25 per cent of the Gross National product. These workers do not appear in official statistics, and this fact explains strange phenomena such as one in Naples, a city which officially has not a single glove factory and yet produces 2 million pairs of gloves annually—a true miracle, Italian style.

Perhaps even more striking and perplexing is the fact that a country with 2.8 million unemployed, a country which traditionally has been exporting its labour to the furthest corners of the world, is today host to over 2 million immigrants, employed in jobs that no

Italian wants to take because they are too heavy or too dangerous or too poorly paid. In 2002 the two largest foreign communities were the Moroccans (119 000) and the Albanians (63 000). Thus Polish miners work in Sardinia, Libyan peasants till the land in Sicily, Tunisian and Moroccan fishermen crew Italian trawlers in the Mediterranean, 100 000 Philippine, Eritrean and Somali women are employed as domestics in Italian families, Egyptians work in the foundries of the Emilio region, Ghanaians harvest tomatoes in Campania. Like Italian migrants who in the past went to distant lands and were welcomed with hostility, racism and sometimes violence, the *extracomunitari*, people coming from countries outside the European Union, are today facing overt racism on the part of some sectors of Italian society. Notable was the despicable outburst of the Mayor of Treviso (nowadays one of the wealthiest provinces in Italy, as well as being, paradoxically, the birthplace of over 600 000 emigrants), who in August 2002 lashed out against a group of homeless Moroccans, describing them as people 'who until recently were hunting lions and gazelles', who were 'watering down the Piave race [i.e. the Italian race]', and who 'should be deported in sealed railway wagons'.

Obviously the labour-hungry Italian economic system is today absorbing foreign unskilled labour as in the past other economies attracted Italian migrants to their factories, mines and assembly lines. In 1997, according to census statistics, of the 986 000 *extracomunitari* legally registered with Italian authorities, only 166 000 had found a job, the remainder being employed in *lavoro nero* or still seeking employment. For this reason, the prevalent image of an Italy beset by instability, poverty and migration contrasts sharply with the reality of the rapid industrial and technological development which in the last fifty years has transformed the country from a basically agricultural nation into an industrial giant.

Today, Italy ranges fifth in armament sales, from the electronics of the Selenia company to the missiles of the Oto-Melara company, from the world-renowned Lupo class frigates to the tanks, guns and aeroplanes of the Fiat industrial complex, or the helicopters of the Agusta company. One hundred and twenty companies are involved in the production of armaments, 60 per cent of which are exported, and employ 70 000 workers. In 1983 this industry had a turnover of 7400 billion lire and recorded a growth rate of 30 per cent.

Italian design is world-renowned. The brands Gucci, Armani, Versace, Ferrè, Dolce and Gabbana dominate international fashion and have even reached the prestigious front page of *Time* magazine, while the names of car designers are synonymous with quality and excellence. From 1980 to 1997 the value of Italian exports rose by 508.1 per cent, against an increase in imports of 314.3 per cent, although, significantly, the advantage gained was lost by a concurrent massive jump in internal consumption. This is an indication that Italians are not prepared to lower their standard of living or to renounce their welfare economy, nor can they be forced to change their lifestyle by a disgracefully inert political system. Incidentally, the balance of trade on goods and services between Italy and Australia in 2001–2 was clearly in favour of Italy, with exports totalling $3892 million and imports of only $2350 million.

According to official 1997 statistics, the average Italian family earns an annual income of approximately 40 million lire, which is often supplemented by *lavoro nero* earnings, which in December 2002 Prime Minister Berlusconi imprudently called *lavoretto non ufficiale* (unofficial little cosy job). With a domestic cost of living lower than Australia's, this income affords comparable purchasing power with the average Australian family. Often, as in Australia, the wife also goes to work to supplement the family income as well as to find a new outlet for her independence and identity. The school, the kindergarten, the social assistance sector and industry are traditional areas of employment for women.

Today, Italian families are more concerned with issues less fundamental than physical survival (such as food and the job) than in the past. A good indicator of it is that, out of 3349.277 lire spent monthly by the average Italian family, only 705.482 lire are spent on food. Quality of life, the contact with and appreciation of nature, pollution, the education of their children, the strengthening of the *privato*—of those personal values such as family, friends, and the local community—are some of the issues which are more topical at present. Urbanisation and the marked improvement in economic conditions have also brought about an understandably wide-ranging change in the social attitudes of Italians.

The secularisation of society has weakened the traditional relationship that Italians had with the Church and the family and revolutionised their morals and attitudes on issues such as divorce, abortion and the pill. The Church, although outwardly still the bulwark of religious practice in its most charismatic manifestations (French historian Jacques Le Goff has characterised the present Pope, John Paul II, as 'the Middle Ages plus television'), as well as the defender of what for centuries was called 'public morality', is seeing its influence waning at an alarming pace. The legalising of divorce in 1974, of abortion in 1975 and the Church's stubborn refusal—on theological grounds—to allow Roman Catholics to use the pill, have alienated many Italians from the Church. A recent survey carried out in the north revealed that a mere 6 per cent of the persons interviewed were practising Roman Catholics. Also, the Church is currently experiencing a dramatic shortage of vocations to the priesthood.

Inter-family relations are today more liberal than thirty or forty years ago. The traditional strict control exercised by the family over their daughters, the custom of chaperoning them until marriage, is a thing of the past and, paradoxically, persists only among those Italians in Australia who still retain this tradition. The economic boom of the 1960s had as one of its main effects the democratisation of education. From then on education was no longer denied to people who could not afford it. The universities were opened to anyone who wanted to study. This measure, taken mainly because the government of the day could not create enough jobs to absorb the post-war baby boom then entering the labour force, lowered the standard of education and at the same time created social discontent among the masses of unemployable, highly educated Italian youth.

The turmoil generated by the failure of a succession of Christian Democrat governments to meet the pressing and rising social aspirations of a society undergoing rapid change was exacerbated by the trend, blindly followed by government, trade unions and political parties alike, of protecting people in official employment and, conversely, of neglecting to protect the rights of the young, of the unemployed, of the underprivileged, of women, of people employed in the *lavoro nero* system. This policy created a division within Italian society, by increasing the gap between the haves and have-nots, by institutionalising the existence of two distinct societies. The ensuing unrest in the 1970s and 1980s degenerated into political terrorism and common criminality. It is well known that the Red Brigades movement began at the University of Trento, where their historical leader, Renato Curcio, was teaching sociology, and that the majority of its members were middle-class intellectuals.

The Red Brigades terrorism, which peaked in the killing of former Prime Minister Aldo Moro in 1978, forced Italians to take stock of the social conditions which alienated unemployed Italian youth, but the success of the mass trials held in Rome, Milan and Turin of up to 161 terrorists, and a growing public disgust, have all but defused

Former Prime Minister Aldo Moro photographed by the Red Brigades while in captivity. (The Economist)

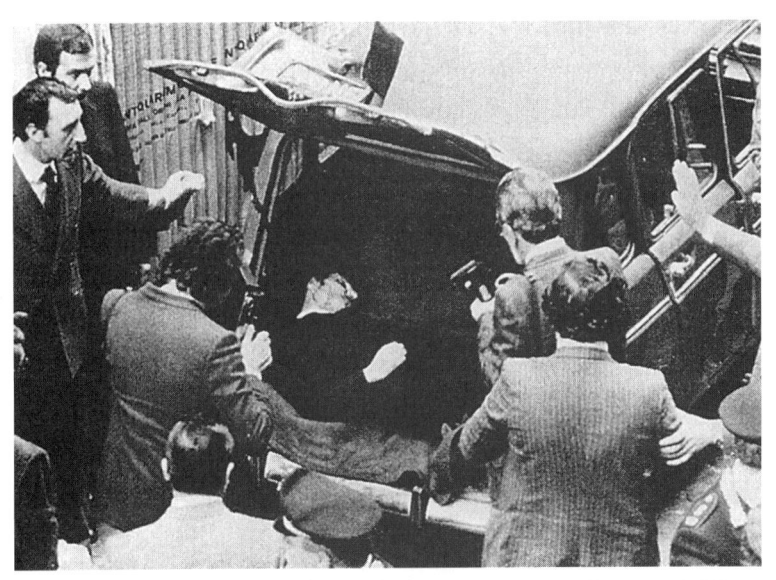

The body of Aldo Moro, murdered by the Red Brigades, found in a car in Via Caetani, Rome. (L'Espresso, 1984)

Renato Curcio, the historical leader of the Red Brigades. (L'Espresso)

the violent reactions that are the tip of the iceberg of social restlessness which pervades Italian society. At present, a university degree in Italy is still not the key to finding a job, but rather a ticket to permanent unemployment and to *lavoro nero*. Today, Italy's youth are the best-educated unemployed in Europe. Even so, with the financial support of the family, with *lavoro nero* and with a generous social security system, life is still more bearable in Italy than in a foreign country.

So nowadays Italians emigrate no more. Understandably, they prefer to stay home, and the historical period during which Italy's main item of export was her unskilled people has ended. As Mario Gargano, a former Italian Deputy Minister for Employment, declared, 'Italians want a job, they do not want to work'. Today, Italy sends abroad different kinds of migrants: engineers, technicians, managers, consultants, people who generally do not suffer from the personal and traumatic experience of emigrating, from social dislocation and alienation, economic exploitation or from the racial and political discrimination endured by the less fortunate Italians who left their homeland in previous times.

Today, Italian migrants no longer come to Australia, where the ageing Italian community—in 1996 almost a third (31.2 per cent) were aged 65 and over, while another third (36.9 per cent) were aged between 50 and 64—remains locked in what Polish writer Jerzy Kosinski aptly called 'the prison of their language and of the claustral sub-culture of emigration'. Thus the bulk of the 218 000

A group of Red Brigadists on trial in Milan. (Courtesy Giovanna Borgese, *Un paese in tribunale*, Mondadori, 1983)

Italian-born migrants and their 582 000 Australian-born children, who, according to the 2001 census, are resident in Australia, are largely unaware of the momentous progress achieved by the Italian people in the last fifty years. They have been bypassed by history.

Their image of Italy is that of the country they left fifty or more years ago. Their code of ethics, of social interaction, of material values and political participation, even of religious worship, which they brought with them when they migrated, is today as unrecognisable in Italy as it is alien to the Australian environment. Their Italian cultural baggage contains mainly pre-industrial development, pre-mass media, and pre-consumerist elements. The dichotomy which exists between them and their children is a case in point. Not only are they unable to understand the values and habits of Australian society which have been accepted by their children, but they are also incapable of imposing on their sons and daughters the observance of their old Italian traditions. This conflict generates a sense of loss of parental authority and dignity, especially when the parents often depend on their children for interpreting and understanding English in shops, hospitals and public offices.

Many cannot grasp and master the complexity of a modern, pluralist, lay, uninhibited urban-industrial society, and they withdraw to the folds of the two structures which for centuries have been the traditional pivots of Italian peasant life: the Church and the village clan. This is why religious celebrations, processions and memorial services on the one hand and social gatherings at regional clubs on the other are such an important aspect of the life of the Italian migrant in Australia. The Catholic Church is still the channel—nowadays the only one—which propounds the values cherished by older Italian migrants in the midst of a largely secular society. The church is still a meeting place, where the most important events in one's life—baptisms, weddings, funerals—can be shared with members of the same village, with fellow migrants or with other *paesani*.

Likewise, regional clubs serve as meeting places for people of the same village or region. They are places where Italian migrants can meet on an equal footing with Australian patrons, without being inhibited by language or social barriers. In a way, the Italian club in Australia is not just the equivalent of the Australian pub, but also the substitute for the Italian village *piazza*, where every evening, every weekend, people meet, socialise, drink, gossip and arrange business and social deals.

Migration is always a traumatic experience, even when it is to a country which has solicited people to come and has accepted them, as Australia has done. It is an agonising experience because the

New Australians. Migrants from the Calabria region dance the Tarantella on board the MV Cyrenia, *bound for Sydney, July 1961.* (Mitchell Library, Sydney)

Italian migrants arrive in Australia in the 1970s. (Cresciani Collection)

migrant leaves not only his country, his city, his friends and his traditions, but also because he leaves behind part of himself. He becomes a stranger in a different—and often indifferent—environment. He feels isolated, defenceless, and vulnerable. He needs to acquire a new sense of identity. He needs security not only in material things, but also, and especially, in his cultural life. He needs to feel accepted by his hosts as a human being, not dehumanised by being told to 'assimilate' as if he were a non-person, an object or factory fodder.

Ultimately, migration represents a moral as well as a political challenge both for the migrant and for his Australian host. It is a test for the migrant, because he has to assert his rights and has to fight for them; for the Australian, because he must understand and accept the fact that every new migrant coming to Australia inexorably and irretrievably changes the character of this country, and ultimately changes him as well.

Only when tolerance towards difference, equality of opportunity, and uninhibited political and social participation in the life of the nation are universally shared values shall we be able to claim Australia as the land of the free, as the song says, and not just a spiritually second-class country, where everybody is, anyhow, a New Australian. Only then shall we be able proudly to proclaim that by settling here, in the newest of the continents, and by combating prejudice and ignorance, by working together for peace and prosperity, by the steadfastness of our labour, sacrifices and achievements, have we prepared the ground and made our contribution to the spiritual as well as to the material development of Australia, to the creation of a civilised society at the Antipodes.

SELECT BIBLIOGRAPHY

Archival material
Archivio Centrale dello Stato, Rome, Direzione Generale di Pubblica Sicurezza, Casellario Politico Centrale (selected *buste*).
Archivio Centrale dello Stato, Rome, Commissariato Generale per l'Emigrazione (selected *buste*).
Australian Archives, Canberra, several government departments (selected files).
Jesuit Archives, Hawthorn, Vic. (selected files).
Ministero degli Affari Esteri, Rome, Archivio Storico-diplomatico (selected *buste*).
New Norcia Mission, Western Australia (selected files).
Sacred Congregation de Propaganda Fide, Rome, Scritture riferite delle Congregazioni Generali, vol. 493, fol. 242.
State Archives of New South Wales, NSW Police Department (selected files).
State Library of New South Wales, Mitchell Collection (selected files).

Published government material
Australian Bureau of Statistics, Canberra, Census 1996 and Census 2001 data.
Australian Bureau of Statistics, Canberra, McDonald, Peter (ed.), *Community Profiles. 1996 Census. Italy Born*, 1999.
Istituto Nazionale di Statistica, *Annuario Statistico Italiano*, Rome, 1998.

Books and essays
Asor Rosa, Alberto, *Le due società. Ipotesi sulla crisi italiana*, Einaudi, Torino, 1977.

AAVV, *Ragguagli delle cose dell'Australia a cominciare dell'anno 1853, compilati sopra i materiali raccolti da una società che prepara una spedizione toscana per le miniere aurifere di quella regione*, Tipografia Galileiana, Firenze, 1853.
Barthes, Roland, *Miti d'oggi*, Einaudi, Torino, 1974.
Bevege, Margaret, *Behind Barbed Wire: Internment in Australia during World War II*, University of Queensland Press, Brisbane, 1993.
Bosworth, Richard, *Italy, The Least of the Great Powers: Italian Foreign Policy before the First World War*, Cambridge University Press, 1979.
Bosworth, Richard and Margot Melia (eds), *Western Australia as it is Today 1906. Leopoldo Zunini Royal Consul of Italy*, University of Western Australia Press, Perth, 1997.
Bosworth, Richard and Janis Wilton, *Old Worlds and New Australia: The Post-war Migrant Experience*, Penguin Books, Melbourne, 1984.
Bosworth, Richard, *Mussolini*, Arnold, London, 2002.
Bosworth, Richard and Michal Bosworth, *Fremantle's Italy*, Gruppo Editoriale Internazionale, Rome, 1993.
Campbell, Eric, *The Rallying Point: My Story of the New Guard*, Melbourne University Press, 1965.
Carboni, Raffaello, *The Eureka Stockade*, Melbourne University Press, 1969.
Cook, James, *Storia dei viaggi intrapresi per ordine di S.M. Britannica dal capitano Giacomo Cook ricavata dalle autentiche relazioni del medesimo*, Ignatio Soffietti Stampatore, Torino 1791.
Cresciani, Gianfranco, *Fascism, Anti-Fascism and Italians in Australia 1922–1945*, Australian National University Press, Canberra, 1980.
Cresciani, Gianfranco, 'The Making of a New Society: Francesco Sceusa and the Italian Intellectual Reformers in Australia 1876–1906'. In John Hardy (ed.), *Stories of Australian Migration*, New South Wales University Press, Sydney, 1988.
Cresciani, Gianfranco, 'Lo spettro della Quinta Colonna italiana in Australia: 1939–1942', in *Affari Sociali Internazionali*, Milano, n. 4, 1985. In English, as 'The Bogey of the Italian Fifth Column: Internment and the Making of Italo-Australia'. In Richard Bosworth and Romano Ugolini (eds), *War, Internment and Mass Migration: The Italo-Australian Experience 1940–1990*, Gruppo Editoriale Internazionale, Rome, 1992.
Cresciani, Gianfranco, 'Captivity in Australia: The Case of Italian Prisoners of War. 1940–1947', in *Studi Emigrazione*, n. 94, 1989.
Cresciani, Gianfranco, *Migrants or Mates. Italian Life in Australia*, Knockmore Enterprises, Sydney, 1988.
De Amicis, Edmondo, *Sull'oceano*, Fratelli Treves, Milano, 1902.
Dignan, Don, 'Chiaffredo Venerano Fraire, 1852–1931'. In Maximilian Brändle, *The Queensland Experience: The Life and Work of 14 Remarkable Migrants*, Phoenix Publications, Brisbane, 1991.

Douglass, William, *From Italy to Ingham: Italians in North Queensland*, University of Queensland Press, Brisbane, 1995.

Fitzgerald, Alan, *The Italian Farming Soldiers: Prisoners of War in Australia 1941–1947*, Melbourne University Press, 1981.

Franzina, Emilio, *L'immaginario degli emigranti: Miti e raffigurazioni dell'esperienza italiana all'estero fra i due secoli*, PAGFVS Edizioni, Treviso, 1992.

Franzina, Emilio, *La grande emigrazione. L'esodo dei rurali dal Veneto durante il secolo XIX*, Marsilio, Venezia, 1976.

Galli, Giorgio, *Il bipartitismo imperfetto. Comunisti e Democristiani in Italia*, Mondadori, Milano, 1984.

Garibaldi, Giuseppe, *Memorie*, Rizzoli, Milano, 1982.

Gilioli, Enrico, *I Tasmaniani: Cenni storici ed etnologici di un popolo estinto*, Fratelli Treves Editori, Milano, 1874.

Ginsborg, Paul, *A History of Contemporary Italy: Society and Politics 1943–1988*, Penguin Books, London, 1990.

Hall, Rodney, *J.S. Manifold. An Introduction to the Man and his Work*, University of Queensland Press, Brisbane, 1978.

Iacini, Stefano, *I risultati della inchiesta agraria (1884)*, Einaudi, Torino, 1976.

Korzelinski, Seweryn, *Memoirs of Gold-Digging in Australia*, University of Queensland Press, Brisbane, 1979.

Levi, Carlo, *Cristo si è fermato a Eboli*, Mondadori, Milano, 1960.

Mack Smith, Denis, *Italy: A Modern History*, University of Michigan Press, Ann Arbor, 1959.

Mack Smith, Denis, *Vittorio Emanuele II*, Laterza, Bari, 1975.

Mack Smith, Denis, *Storia della Sicilia medievale e moderna*, Laterza, Bari, 1976.

Matvejević, Predrag, *Mediterraneo. Un nuovo breviario*, Garzanti, Milano, 1999.

Mitchell, Thomas, *Viaggi nell'interno dell'Australia o Nuova Olanda*, Tipografia Giachetti, Prato, 1844.

Molinari, Augusta, *Le navi di Lazzaro. Aspetti sanitari dell'emigrazione transoceanica italiana: il viaggio per mare*, Franco Angeli, Milano, 1988.

Moore, Andrew, *The Secret Army and the Premier: Conservative Paramilitary Organisations in New South Wales 1930–32*, New South Wales University Press, Sydney, 1989.

Moore, Bob and Kent Fedorowich, *The British Empire and its Italian Prisoners of War, 1940–1947*, Palgrave, New York, 2002.

Niau, Josephine, *The Phantom Paradise: The Story of the Expedition of the Marquis De Rays*, Angus & Robertson, Sydney 1936.

O'Grady, John, *They're a Weird Mob*, Ure Smith, Sydney, 1974.

Procacci, Giuliano, *History of the Italian People*, Penguin Books, London, 1968.
Rosoli, Gianfausto, *Insieme oltre le frontiere: Momenti e figure dell'azione della Chiesa tra gli emigrati italiani nei secoli XIX e XX*, Salvatore Sciascia Editore, Caltanissetta, 1996.
Salvado, Rudesindo, *Memorie storiche dell'Australia, particolarmente della missione benedettina di Nuova Norcia e degli usi e costumi degli australiani*, Tipografia Vincenzo Priggiobba, Napoli, 1852.
Tomasi di Lampedusa, Giuseppe, *Il Gattopardo*, Feltrinelli, Milano, 1962.
Thompson, Roger, *Australian Imperialism in the Pacific: The Expansionist Era 1820–1920*, Melbourne University Press, 1980.
Ware, Helen, *A Profile of the Italian Community in Australia*, Citadel Press, Melbourne, 1981.

Films
Turkiewicz, Sophia (Director), *Silver City*, Screnplay co-written by Thomas Keneally, produced by Simpson, Darren, 1984.

Journals and newspapers
Age, Melbourne
Balmain Observer, Sydney
Bondi Daily, Sydney
Bulletin, Sydney
Corriere della Sera, Milano
Il Risveglio, Sydney
Italo-Australian, Sydney
La Repubblica, Milano
La Riscossa, Melbourne and Ingham
L'Espresso, Milano
Herald, Melbourne
Newsweek
Oceania, Sydney
Smith's Weekly, Sydney
Sun, Sydney
Sydney Morning Herald
The Economist, London
Time Magazine
Uniamoci, Sydney
Worker, Sydney

INDEX

Aborigines 29, 30, 41
Abruzzi 7
Achin Bay 32
Adelaide 30
Adenauer, Konrad 154
Adriatic 121
Africa 13, 23, 26
Age, The 41
Agreement for Cultural Co-operation between Italy and Australia 145
Aigues Mortes, lynching of Italians 23
Alberoni, Francesco 146
Alps 1, 13
Ambrosoli, Angelo 30
Amelia 41
Amendola, Giovanni 78
American Press, articles on Italy 155
An 42
Andrea Doria 23
Andreotti, Giulio 144, 153, 154, 156, 159, 160
Anglo-Maersk 99
Antico, Giovanni Terribile 139
Antico, Sir Tristan 139
Antonini, Rev. Dr Michele 30
Anzac Day 83
Apulia 161
Aquila 41
Arena, Franca 117, 135–6
Arena, L. 40
Argentina 14, 19, 23
Armando Diaz 93
Armati, Pio Vico 43, 47
Armidale 32

Armosino, Francesca 3
Art Gallery of New South Wales 146
Ascom 136, 166
Asia 26
Asor Rosa, Alberto 146
Aspromonte 3
Asselin, Gian Carlo 38
Assisted Migration Agreement 125
Atlas 99
Atrevida 28
Aulenti, Gae 148
Australia 24
  Army Intelligence 97
  Federation 51
Australian attitudes
  towards Italian migrants 40–1, 52, 96
  towards Italy 68–70
Australian Museum, Sydney 147
Australian Research Council 145
Australian Workers' Union 67, 68
Austria
  Army 7, 10, 11, 13
  Navy 10
  political influence of 7

Bakunin, Mickhail Aleksandrovic 1
Ballarat 38
Balmain Observer 101
Baltic Sea 121
Bandiera brothers, Attilio and Emilio 14
Baracchi, Pietro 39
Barthes, Roland 141
Bass Strait 33, 45
Batavia 32

INDEX

Batchiane 42
Battistessa, Franco 79, 84
Bava-Beccaris, Fiorenzo 12
Belgiorno-Nettis, Franco 137, 138, 166
Belgium 19, 97, 164
Bellini, Mario 148
Benso, Camillo, Count of Cavour 11, 12, 13
Bentivoglio, Carlo 47
Benvenuti 43
Berlin Wall 155
Berlusconi, Silvio 153, 157, 158, 170
Bernacchi, Angelo Giulio Diego 39, 45
Bernacchi, Barbe 45
Biagi, Giuseppe 37
Bicentenary celebrations 146
Biella 8
Bismarck Archipelago 43
Bixio, Nino 32
Boccelli, Andrea 146
Bodei, Remo 146
Boers 33
Bolshevik Revolution 75
Bombelli, Stefano 29
Bondi Daily 101
Bonegilla 128, 130, 135
Borghese, Junio Valerio 126
Borneo 42
Borsellino, Paolo 160
Bossi, Umberto 157, 158, 162
Botany Bay 28
Boulder 58, 79
Bourbons 7, 14
Brambilla, Fernando 29
Branca, Vittore 146
Brazil 14, 19, 23
Brisbane 30, 60, 99
British Preference League 68
Broad Arrow 58
Broken Hill 63, 79
Broken Hill Proprietary Company 136
Bruce, Stanley Melbourne 69, 89
Bruxner, Michael 102
Bulletin 57
Bulong 58
Buoninsegni-Vitali, Luigi 84
Burgess, Marie 38
Byron, George Gordon, Lord 1, 8

Cachar 23
Calabria 161
Calabria 52
Calwell, Arthur Augustus 125
Camerino 47
Camorra 159, 161, 164
Campania 161
Campbell, Eric 92
Canada 24, 121, 123
Canali, Giuseppe 43
Canberra 57
Cane cutters' strikes 90
Caporelli, Nicola 30
Capra, Giuseppe 60, 61, 62
Carabinieri 78, 160
Caracciolo 42
Carandini, Girolamo, Count 38
Carboni, Raffaello 34, 38
Carlo Raggio 23
Carmagnola, Francesco Giuseppe 86, 87, 88, 89, 90, 94, 95
Carmen 33
Carosi, Mario 84, 85
Carrara Marble Works 41
Carso 74
Cassa del Mezzogiorno 162–3
Cassamarca Foundation 146
Cassino 163
Castello di Rivoli Museo d'Arte Contemporanea, Turin 147
Catani, Ugo 39
Catholicism 75
Cattaneo, Bartolomeo 84
Cerruti, Emilio 42
Changi 111
Charles VIII of France 119
Chartists 9
China 27, 41
Churchill, Winston 121, 153
Circolo Isole Eolie 60
Club Cavour, Melbourne 64
Coburg 139
Coburg Peninsula 30
Colditz 111
Cold War 121, 155
Colombo, Cristoforo 28
Coltano 111
Commonwealth Police 86
Como 45
Confalonieri, Angelo 30
Congregation for the Propagation of the Faith 28, 29
Cook, Captain James 27, 28
Cooktown 30
Coonabarabran 114

Corrimal 79
Corruption, political 157–9
Corte, Pasquale 48, 56, 60
Cossiga, Francesco 144
Cosulich Line 20
Cowra 107, 111, 113, 114
Craxi, Bettino 156
Crimean War 13
Cristoforo Colombo 42
Cue 58
Curcio, Renato 160, 172, 174
Custoza 10
Czechoslovakia 144

Dachau 111
Dalla Chiesa, Carlo Alberto 160
Dal Monte, Toti 70, 71
Danieli, Franco 141
Dante Alighieri Society 60
Dardanelli, Bartolomeo 40
Darlington 45
Darwin, Japanese bombing of 123
Davadi, Girolamo 31
Day Down 58
Daylesford 34, 35
De Amicis, Edmondo 53
De Felice, Renzo 146
De Gasperi, Alcide 125, 153, 161
De Groot, Francis Edward, Captain 91, 92
De Marco, Divo 47
De Mauro, Tullio 146
De Muro Lomanto, Enzo 70, 71
De Pinedo, Francesco 69, 70
De Rays, Marquis Charles Du Breil 43–4
Del Drago, Prince Alfonso 104
Del Pin, Eustacchio 81, 82
Denmark 97
Descubierta 28
Dini, Lamberto 145
Di Pietro, Antonio 156
Dodecanese Islands 27
Downer, Alexander 145
Dubček, Alexandr 144
Duhig, Archbishop James 84, 92
Dunne, Archbishop Robert 31

Eco, Umberto 146
Egypt 108
Eisenhower, Dwight David 154
Eldorado 19, 23
Electric Power Transmission 136, 166
Ellis Island 23
Emilia 7
Enlightenment 26
Ercole, Quinto 47
Eritrea 24, 27
Ethiopia 27, 92
Etna 42
Eureka Stockade revolt 38
Europe
  reconstruction of 24
  refugees 121–3
European Economic Community 25, 165
European Recovery Plan 161

Fabiani, Fabrizio 40
Falcone, Giovanni 160
Fanfani, Amintore 153
Fantin, Francesco 105
Federation of Italian Workers and their Families (FILEF) 144
Felce 99
Ferrante, Agostino 91
Ferrara 4
Ferry Report 67
Ferry, Thomas A. 67, 70
Festa dello Statuto 61
Fiaschi, Tommaso 39
FIAT Industries 24, 163, 170
Fiocchi, Adalgiso 47
First Fleet 28
First World War 102
Florence 4, 5, 121, 160
Fortini, Monsignor Paolo 30
Fraire, Chiaffredo Venerano 43, 47
France 6, 11, 13, 19, 23, 24, 41, 87, 96, 97, 164
Fraser, Malcolm 25, 144
Frederick May Foundation for Italian Studies, Sydney 146
Fremantle 39, 60, 99
Fulton 121

Galli, Giorgio 154
Garden Palace, Sydney 48
Gargano, Mario 174
Garibaldi claim 34
Garibaldi, Giuseppe 3, 11, 13, 14, 32, 48
  in Australia 33
Garibaldi, Giuseppe (Peppino) 33
Garibaldi Legion 33

INDEX

Garibaldi, Ricciotti 33
Gela 162
Gelmetti, Gianluigi 148
Geneva Convention 100–1, 116
Genoa 5, 9, 14, 23, 32, 41, 163
Gentile, Emilio 146
Germany, 19, 41, 77, 98, 164
  internment policy of 98
  military defeat of 119
Ghibellines 5
Giglioli, Enrico Hillyer 41
Gilroy, Cardinal Sir Norman 84, 93
Giorgetti, Samuele 39
Giuliano, Boris 160
Giunta, Francesco 76
Gladio-Stay Behind organisation 156
Gobbo, Sir James 138
Gobetti, Piero 78
Goethe, Johann Wolfgang von 1
Goffredo Mameli 32, 40, 41
Gold Rush and Italians 34–8
Good Neighbour Council 132
Gorki, Maxim 1
Gorlier, Claudio 146
Gramsci, Antonio 16
Granville, Second Earl of 42
Grassby, Al 127, 140, 141
Great Britain, 13, 27, 41, 42, 43, 51, 96, 97, 98
  emigration from 2
  internment policy of 98
Great Depression 67, 71, 89, 91
Greece 3, 33
Greta 128
Griffith 65, 68, 79
Grocon Constructions 136, 137, 166
Grollo, brothers Bruno and Rino 137, 145
Grollo, Luigi 137
Grossardi, Antonio 82, 86
Guelphs 5
Guevara, Ernesto ('Che') 13

Halifax 80
Hannibal 1
Hanson, Pauline 149
Hay 99, 107, 113
Herald (Melbourne) 41
Herbert, Robert 40
Hitler, Adolf 1, 77, 92, 119, 120
Hobart 38, 45
Hreščák, Iacob 8

Immigration policy 40–1, 168–9
Immigration Restriction Act, 1901 55, 57
India 50, 112, 121, 153
India 44
Indonesia 154
Industrial Revolution 26
Ingham 67, 89, 90
International Exhibitions in Australia 34, 42
International Red Cross 108
International Socialist Congress, Zurich, 1893 48
Interpol 48
Italian anti-Fascism, 80, 84–5, 95
  Australian attitudes towards 94
  demonstrations 80, 88–91, 94
  in Queensland 89
  Russell Street fight 89
Italian Australian Institute, Melbourne 145
Italian Australian Records Project, Melbourne 145
Italian Chambers of Commerce 148
Italian Committee of Assistance (Co-As-It) 145
Italian Fascism
  appeal to migrants 81, 83, 92
  Australian attitudes towards 91–2, 94–5, 98
  Catholic Church support of 75, 84, 91, 92
  collapse of 120–1
  Fascist branches in
    Adelaide 82
    Melbourne 81, 82, 83
    Sydney 85, 91, 93, 104
  Fascist propaganda 81, 84, 92, 93
  Fascist violence 75, 78
  imperialism 92
  Italian Ex Servicemen's Association 104
  March on Rome 76, 77, 89
  Opera Volontaria Repressione Antifascismo (OVRA) 86
  rise of 1, 24, 74, 75–7
Italian Historical Society, Melbourne 138, 145
Italian Institute of Culture 145
Italian Institute of Statistics (ISTAT) 3, 167

Italian migrants in Australia 178
  assimilation of 70, 72, 98, 150
  Catholic Church and 3, 147, 176–7
  celebrations 83, 140, 143
  Census data 141–3
  conditions of employment 35, 36, 37, 49, 53, 55, 56, 58, 59, 67–8, 135, 136, 138
  culture shock 50, 63, 128
  differences between Italians 5
  disturbances 128–30
  Fifth Column 71, 98, 103, 106
  hostility against 23, 57–8, 62, 70–1, 102
  illiteracy 55, 60, 62
  internment 100
  internment camps 101
  internment statistics 100, 105
  isolation and alienation 60–1, 62–4, 132–3
  Italian welfare societies in Australia 47, 60
  Little Italies 58, 139
  living conditions 71–2, 80, 132, 176
  marriages 49, 133
  migrant hostels 128, 131, 137
  occupations of interned Italians 104
  perception of Italy 105–6
  political affiliations 47, 94
  social clubs 139, 177
  statistics 54, 78, 100, 167
  strike breaking 63–4
  women 133
Italian political parties 156–7
Italian prisoners of war in Australia, 99
  Australian attitudes to 116–18
  concentration camps for 102, 107–8, 109, 121
  conditions in camps 108–9, 111, 116
  contacts with civilians 110, 114–15
  Directorate of Prisoners of War 110
  economic contribution to war effort of 107, 111, 116–18
  escapes by 113
  Farm Release Scheme 110, 114
  health of 109, 111–13, 116
  murders 105
  repatriation of 116
  statistics 107, 110
  Trade Union attitudes towards 110
Italian Workers' Welfare Society 47, 60

Italo-Australian 80
Italo-Australiano 62
Italy
  abortion 171
  armaments industry 170
  Army 14, 16, 47
  beginning of mass migration 16, 18, 19, 20, 22
  brigandage 6, 16
  Christian Democratic Party 82, 153, 154
  Church and family 171
  colonial policy 41–3, 52
  Commissariat General for Emigration 51–2, 54, 61
  Communist Party 144, 155
  conditions on board migrant ships 21, 22, 53, 177
  consequences of military defeat 24, 119
  consumerism 162
  Counter Reformation 8
  declaration of war 15, 97, 101
  dialects 7
  economic depressions 19–21
  economic miracle 25, 161–2
  end of emigration from 25, 140, 175–6
  establishment of diplomatic relations with Australia 39–40
  fashion and design 170
  First World War 20, 64, 66, 73
  foreign migrants in 25, 168
  industrialisation 8, 9, 162
  internal migration 24, 165
  Kingdom of 13
  lavoro nero 168, 170, 172, 174
  migration policy to Australia 51–2
  nationalist propaganda 63–4, 75
  patronage system 162–4, 167
  peasants 10, 13, 16
  peasant unrest 12, 14, 16, 73–4
  Reformation 7
  remittances to 19
  Renaissance 3, 152
  Resistance movement 120
  Socialist Party 47, 56
  socio-economic conditions today 164–5, 171–2, 174
  Southern question 4
  stability of political system 152–5
  Statute of the Workers 167

INDEX

stereotypes of 4, 155
tourists 3
trade unions 19, 73, 85
unemployment 168
Unification 4, 6, 7, 9, 10, 11, 12, 13, 14, 16, 19, 27, 33, 40

Japan 161
John Paul II, Pope 171
Joyce, James 1

Kalgoorlie, 58, 61, 79
  Riots 1919 66–7
  Riots 1934 61, 68
Kanaka labour in Queensland 45, 46, 56
Kanowna 58
Ke 42
Keats, John 1
Kelly, Ned 50
Keneally, Thomas 128
Kent 40
Khrushchev, Nikita Sergeyevich 154
Kipling, Rudyard 52
Korzelinski, Seweryn 34
Kosinski, Jerzy 175
Kremlin 154

Labor Party, 91
  hostility towards Italian migrants 55–8
Lane, William 57
Lang, Jack 92
Laverton 58
Lazio 7
Leeton 114
Lefebvre, Archbishop Marcel 1
Legambiente 160–1
Legge Cirami 158
Le Goff, Jacques 171
Leichhardt 139
Lenin, Vladimir Ilic 1
Lennonville 58
Leonora 58
Levi, Carlo 50
Liberalism 26
Libia 93
Libya 24, 27
Lidia 41
Lima, Salvatore 160
Lismore, NSW 45, 61, 79
Lissa 10

Lithgow 79
Liverpool 128
Lombardy 6, 45, 47
London 10
Long Bay Jail 100
Lorraine, House of 7
Loveday 105, 108, 111
Lozza 45
Luther, Martin 1
Lyons, Joseph Aloysius 89, 91, 93

Mack Smith, Denis 7
Mafia 4, 144, 159, 160, 161, 163, 164
Magenta 41
Magris, Claudio 158
Mair, Alex 102, 103
Malaria 162
Malaspina, Alessandro 28
Manifold, John 100
Manila 28
Mani Pulite 156
Mann, Thomas 1
Mannix, Archbishop Daniel 93
Manoora 99
Mantua 4, 80
Marche 7
Maria Island 45
Marrinup 108
Marsala 14
Marshall, George 161
Martelli, Alessandro 41
Matera 162
Matra, James 28
Matraville 130
Matteo Bruzzo 23
Matteotti Club 87–8, 90, 139
Matteotti, Giacomo 78, 85, 90
Mauritius 41
Mazzini, Giuseppe 11, 14
Melano, Mario 90
Melbourne 34, 37, 39, 40, 41, 42, 45, 47, 60, 67, 68, 79, 89, 93, 94, 137, 145
Menzies, Robert Gordon 97, 98, 100
Metternich, Prince Clemens Wenzel Nepomuk Lothar von 6
Mexico 33
Milan, 4, 24, 47, 121, 123, 146, 163, 168, 172
  riots 12, 47, 74
Minzoni, Giovanni 78
Mitchell, Thomas Livingstone 29

Mitzkievich, Adam 14
Modena 47
Modena, Duchy of 7
Modigliani, Franco 146
Montanelli, Indro 156
Montevideo 23
Morandi, Giorgio 147
Morel, George W. 108, 109
Moro, Aldo 145, 153, 172, 173
Moscow 93
Multicon 136
Multiculturalism 8, 140
Munari, Pietro 47
Murchison 108
Murrumbidgee Irrigation Scheme 65, 66
Museum of Contemporary Art, Sydney 147, 148
Mussolini, Benito Amilcare Andrea 13, 24, 76, 77, 81, 82, 84, 85, 88, 89, 92, 93, 94, 95, 96, 100, 120, 121, 124
Myrtleford 108, 111

Naples 23, 163, 164, 168
Napolitano, Giorgio 167
National Gallery of Victoria 147, 148
'Ndragheta 161
Nehru, Jawaharlal 153
Nerli, Girolamo 39
Netherlands 42, 97
New Britain 45
New Guard 92
New Guinea 42
New Hebrides 45
New Ireland 43
New Italy Settlement 36, 37, 38, 44, 45
New Norcia 30, 31
New Orleans, lynching of Italians 23
New Settlers Association 132
New South Wales 29, 39, 43, 44
New Testament translation for Aborigines 30
New York 23
Nhill 103
Northam 108
North Atlantic Treaty Organisation (NATO) 155
Northern League 153, 157
Norway 97
Novara 10

Oceania 26, 27
Oceania 62
Ockerism 149
Odessa 41
O'Grady, John 149
Old Guard 92
Old Macaroni Factory 35
Olympic Games 2000, Sydney 146
O'Malley, King 57
One Nation Party 149
Opera Bonomelli 17, 61–2
Opera House, Sydney 146
Orange 115

Pact of Steel 97
Padiglione d'Arte Contemporanea, Milan 146
Palermo 28, 159, 160, 164, 168
Pantano, Edoardo 22
Papi 43
Paris 10
Parkes, Sir Henry 45
Parma, Duchy of 7
Parramatta 29
Paul VI, Pope 144
Pearl Harbor 105
Pecorelli, Mino 159
Pentridge Jail 100
Perth 30
Pertini, Sandro 88, 95
Perugia 160
Petöfi, Sandor 14
Petronilla 41
Piano, Renzo 148
Piccinini, Patricia 148
Piedmont, 11, 13, 47
 Army 14
Pioneer Concrete Services 139
Piovene 139
Pisa 4, 5
Pisacane, Carlo 14, 16
Poland 97
Polding, John Bede 29
Porena, Luciano 48
Porta Pia, breach of 5
Port Essington 30
Porto Marghera 24
Portoghesi, Paolo 148
Pound, Ezra 1
Powerhouse Museum, Sydney 147
Prague 144
Prampolini, Giuseppe 47, 62, 63, 72

Principessa Clotilde 42
Procacci, Giuliano 146

Queen Mary 107
Queensland, 43, 45, 47
  anti-Italian sentiment 56–7, 67
Quinn, Bishop James 43

Racchia, Carlo 42
Rahn, Rudolf 124
Raimondo Montecuccoli 93, 94
Ravenet, Giovanni 29
Red Army 155
Red Brigades terrorism 4, 152, 155, 160, 172, 173, 174, 175
Refugees 121–2, 129
Reggio Emilia 24, 148
Remo 99
Revolution, French 7
Ricciarelli, Katia 146
Riccio, Vittorio 28, 29, 50
Richi 43
Riscossa 86, 87, 90
Risorgimento 10, 11, 13, 16, 19
Risveglio 86
Rogerius & Sons 39
Roman Catholic Church
  Concordat 91
  missionaries 27
  Roman Question 27
Rome 1, 3, 12, 13, 27, 28, 38, 43, 60, 61, 69, 76, 87, 93, 94, 120, 162, 168, 172
Romolo 99
Rosina 41
Rossi, Francois 28
Royal Commissions on Italians 57–8
Royal Navy 28
Rubattino, Raffaele, Shipping Line 9
Rumor, Mariano 153
Ruskin, John 1
Russia 121

Salemi, Ignazio 144
Salteri, Carlo 137
Salvado, Bishop Rosendo 30, 31
Salza, Father Giacomo 89
San Diego 45
Santa Cecilia, Orchestra di 146
Saragat, Giuseppe 144
Sardinia, Kingdom of 6, 9, 12, 35, 39
Sartoral, Valentino 129

Savonarola, Girolamo 120, 121
Savoy Dynasty 6
Scalfaro, Oscar Luigi 144
Sceusa, Francesco 47, 48
Schiassi, Omero 17, 79, 85
Schio 47
Scullin, James Henry 89
Shelley, Percy Bysshe 1, 38
Sicilies, Kingdom of the Two 7, 39
Sicily, 13, 14, 161
  conquered by Garibaldi 14
Siegfried 119
Simonetti, Achille 43
Simoni, Edgardo 115
Singapore 42
Smithfield 68
Smith's Weekly 57
Snowy Mountains Hydro Electric Scheme 134
Socialism 75
Socialist movement 19
Socialist Party 153
Società Stella d'Italia 61
Società Umanitaria 17, 61
Soekarno, Achmed 154
Solomon Islands 45
Somalia 24, 27
South Africa 24, 121
South America 14, 87
Southern Cross 58
Soviet Union 77, 155
Spanish Civil War 92, 93
Spence, William 57
Spini, Giorgio 146
Stalin, Josif Vissarionovich Dzugashvili 77
Stanthorpe 31, 67
State Library of New South Wales 145
Stendhal, (Marie-Henri Beyle) 1
Stettin 121
St Ives 67
Stradbroke Island 30
Subiaco 30
Sugarloaf 31
Sumatra 32
Sun, Sydney 101
Sydney 32, 41, 42, 47, 60, 62, 79, 89, 94, 145, 148
  Japanese submarine attack of 123
Sydney Morning Herald 70
Sydney Symphony Orchestra 148
Sylos Labini, Paolo 146

INDEX

Tamworth 115
Tangentopoli 156
Taranto 162
Tasmania 39, 41, 43
Tassa sul macinato 19
Tatura 108
Tenix 166
Teramo 47
Three Hummock Island 33
Tientsin 27
Tittoni, Tommaso 18
Tomasi di Lampedusa, Giuseppe 150
Torregiani, Bishop Elzeario 31, 32
Townsville 47, 90, 99
Transfield, 136, 137–8, 166
   Art Prize 138, 144
   Biennale 138, 144, 166
Transvaal 33, 56
Treaty of Commerce and Navigation, 1883 43
Treaty of London, 1915 64
Trento University 172
Treviso 137, 146
Trieste 15, 76, 121, 122, 127
Turin 12, 24, 47, 163, 172
   Riots 74
Turkiewicz, Sophia 128
Tusa, Giuseppe 28
Tuscany, Grand Duchy of 7, 39

Uffizi Gallery, Florence 160
Umbria 7
Uniamoci 62, 63
Unità 144
United Australia Party 91
United States of America 19, 23, 42, 87, 123, 161
   internment policy 98
   restriction of immigration, 1921 24, 52, 78
University of Sydney 146

Urbino 4
Uruguay 14

Vaccari, Raimondo 30
Vanzetti, Eugenio 39
Vatican 3, 91
Veneto 6, 47, 67, 86
Venezuela 33
Venice 4, 5, 24
Venice Biennale 148
Venturi, Franco 146
Verdi, Giuseppe 38
Veroli, Luigi 41
Vespucci, Amerigo 28
Vettor Pisani 42
Viareggio 39
Victor Emmanuel II, King 11, 12
Victor Emmanuel III, King 76
Victoria 28, 33, 35, 39
Victoria University 145
Vienna, Congress of 6, 10
Villa, Pancho 33
Villawood 128, 130
Von Guerard, Eugene 34

Wagga Wagga 114
Wallangarra 31
Watson, John 57
Weil's disease 90
Western Australia, 33, 63
   anti-Italian sentiment 56
Western Germany 161
White Australia Policy 45
Whitlam, Edward Gough 140, 145
Wiluna 58, 79
Windsor 39
Wonthaggi 79
Woodburn 45
Worker (Brisbane) 68

Yalta, Agreement of 6, 121